BRAND DAMAGE

BRAND DAMAGE

It's Personal!

Larry G. Linne & Patrick Sitkins

authorHOUSE®

AuthorHouse™
1663 Liberty Drive
Bloomington, IN 47403
www.authorhouse.com
Phone: 1-800-839-8640

Published by AuthorHouse   04/29/2013

ISBN: 978-1-4817-4456-0 (sc)
ISBN: 978-1-4817-4460-7 (hc)
ISBN: 978-1-4817-4561-1 (e)

Library of Congress Control Number: 2013907386

Any people depicted in stock imagery provided by Thinkstock are models, and such images are being used for illustrative purposes only.
Certain stock imagery © *Thinkstock.*

This book is printed on acid-free paper.

Because of the dynamic nature of the Internet, any web addresses or links contained in this book may have changed since publication and may no longer be valid. The views expressed in this work are solely those of the author and do not necessarily reflect the views of the publisher, and the publisher hereby disclaims any responsibility for them.

CONTENTS

ACKNOWLEDGMENTS

My first book, *Make the Noise Go Away*, was written due to intense market demand. My clients demanded that I write a book because I couldn't get to all of them. This book was different. I wrote it because I was passionate about it and saw the world shifting.

However, the shifts in my life made writing it very difficult. My businesses are thriving, my kids are growing up and need me around, and my wife likes having me around. The last few years have been a challenge to find the time to write.

I am truly thankful for my family in every way. They are my inspiration, and they challenge me to be the best I can be. I want to be worthy of being their husband and father. I hope this book helps accomplish that goal, as they have all sacrificed in its writing. Debi, you are my best friend. Tiffany, Wen Jun, Macie, Avree, and Lia, you guys are my lifeblood. Thanks for making me the man I am today. I can't wait to see how you will change me in the future.

I also want to thank my clients and friends who gave me the experiences to write about. Books of interest usually have true stories. Thank you for trying our ideas.

Lee Brower, you have inspired me and helped me be a better me. Much gratitude to you my friend.

Mike Natalizio, thanks for bouncing ideas around. You are a branding genius.

Patrick, I admire you for your guts and desire to build your own business. Your generation is powerful and will make landmark changes in our world. This book and your input show just a glimpse of those changes.

Thank you and Di for being great friends and for your endless hours of ideas and writing in this book. We have a lot more to get accomplished. We have to pay for college for your inspiration, Callen and Baby #2!

Roger Sitkins, thank you for providing opportunity.

INTRODUCTION

LARRY LINNE

Twelve years ago I spoke to a group of Canadian and US business executives about the power and importance of personal branding. You would have thought I was communicating blasphemy. The feedback was harsh. It was considered "selfish" to brand yourself. They saw personal branding as something you would do as an actor, athlete, or someone who was trying to draw attention to himself or herself. In a world where teams were the focus of business, it just seemed out of place to allow personal branding to be accepted.

My speech was not well received and was dismissed as a needed business strategy. Over the twelve years since giving this speech, I have continued to manage my personal brand and help individuals who buy into the process. Still, many continued to reject the concept. It wasn't until three years ago that I finally was able to clearly articulate a compelling reason that someone should manage his or her brand.

The trends in the past ten years have naturally swayed toward more acceptance for many reasons we will outline in this book. However, the most compelling reason came from the definition we are using for "brand." A brand is what people think of you. So, when I speak today to business leaders, I ask them to write down what others think of them. I ask them to identify what personal attributes they would most benefit from if those items were well-known to those with whom they interact personally and professionally. Then I reveal to them the truth. If they wrote down anything when asked what others think of them, they have a brand. If they wrote down anything when asked if they had attributes to highlight, they have a "desired brand."

In a recent workshop with a group of fifty salespeople, I had them do this branding exercise. Each of them wrote down what they believed people thought of them. I asked them to include what friends, family, coworkers, and acquaintances may say about them. I encouraged them to write down all positive, negative, and neutral things they believed others would say in an anonymous request to describe what they think of them. After they had written down a list of items, I asked them to write down what they would want people to think of them, if they wanted to get the most out of those relationships. The fifty salespeople were all shocked at how different the first list was from the second. They realized they had allowed others to perceive or focus on certain things about them that were not the most beneficial in their relationships.

Next we discussed how they could have had slightly different behaviors and been more purposeful. The purpose of this discussion was to show them how minor adjustments in their behavior could have made the second list (desired brand) a reality. They could have done little things like participate more proactively in conversations, purposeful choice of dress and appearance on different occasions, and other simple behavior changes. (We will address many of these ideas in the following chapters.)

Many people in the world will say that they feel "misunderstood." Well, I believe it is because they have sent a brand message that is different from the real them.

The buy-in at my speeches and training becomes much stronger when these realities are introduced. When we show them how often they are being researched on the Internet (as individuals) and show people how accessible their brands are, they get really interested in personal brand management. It is my belief that personal brand management is going to be a strategic initiative in all businesses by 2015—if they are to survive.

I am fifty years old and have thirty years of experience in marketing and branding. I have rebranded hundreds of companies and individuals all over North America, Central America, and Latin American. I have applied the principles you will read about in this book to my companies and products (e.g., Sitkins International, Intellectual Innovations, Make the Noise Go Away, Noise Reduction System™, MyExit Strategies™, and more). The results of these companies and products have all been greater than expected because of our ability to manage the brand.

However, I felt the need to bring a younger brand expert into this project. I worked with Patrick Sitkins for six years at Sitkins Group Inc. (under the brand Sitkins International). We have continued to collaborate since he has moved on to his own marketing and branding company, SiliconCloud. I was honored to mentor Patrick for six years of his career. Now he has moved on and has developed skills and understanding around branding that are different and expanded from what I was able to teach him. Patrick is typical of an early thirty-something marketing guy. He is irreverent, smart, fearless in business, and lives to make a difference. We have worked on many branding projects, and the "iron sharpens iron" concept has worked well in our relationship. So you will receive great value throughout this book. The combination of my thirty years of experience in all aspects of branding and Patrick's understanding of modern brand management and technology will provide you with what you need in order to create and manage your personal brand.

The first section of the book will be my thoughts, and Patrick will make comments along the way. The second section of the book will be Patrick's thoughts, and I will make comments in his section. I believe you will find some interesting generational and experiential differences between us. The third section of the book will be the Personal Branding Handbook. This guide will provide insight into how you should think about your brand. It will give you strategies and tactics to build a personal brand that will maximize your success.

We are going to be very vulnerable throughout this book. For us to express what we know about personal branding, we will have to share our own experiences. I almost didn't write this book because of how much I would be exposing of my internal strategies and tactics. Although my intentions are very good, they may be misunderstood. I hope you will honor this trust that Patrick and I are giving you. It is intended to help you. So, how can that be perceived as bad? I promise you will learn something new about branding as you read through this book.

PATRICK SITKINS

Branding? Reputation? Who I am? We might as well bust out the bongo drums, light up the peace pipe, and get a game of Hacky Sack going.

I was discussing personal branding during dinner with one of my clients in New Mexico, and after a few minutes of conversation the CEO of the organization told the rest of the table that we were writing a book on the topic. His wife, Julie, said, "That's great! It's like 'finding yourself' for the business world. You know, discovering who you are without the bonfire, spiritualism, and dope smoking." She was right. A lot of branding is discovering who you are, what value you bring, what your natural talents are, and crafting that into a very clear message.

Branding, as we define it, is what people think of you. In its simplest form, that's what it is. It is the culmination of several complex strategies, interactions, media, communications, experiences, and relationships all boiled down into a very clear and very real opinion of you.

Just as Julie described it, branding is often seen as new age, cushy, or soft, especially in the business world. We may have an easier time convincing professionals to go on a quest to find the pot of gold at the end of a rainbow while riding a unicorn. With all of the opportunities, dangers, and distractions that organizations have, they usually have an extremely hard time understanding the value in focusing on their corporate brand or helping their employees manage theirs. They typically want to focus on items that have a concrete impact on the bottom line. And branding is not traditionally seen as one of those items.

The market is now placing much more stock in individuals than in big corporate brands. In the last few years we have seen huge, powerful, and well-known titans of industry fall. Scandals, bailouts, downsizing, massive layoffs, ethical misconduct, and golden parachutes have dominated the headlines. Consumers have taken notice of all of this. Now, more than ever before, the public has become disenfranchised. Millennials and gen Xers especially have lost faith in corporate structures and messages. They now rely on word of mouth, social groups, recommendations, and strong connections. The individual is now more important than the whole. What people think about you is now more important than who you belong to.

The principles in this book will not only help you see value in personal branding, but more importantly, it will give you strategies to consider and will connect you to resources to help you manage your personal brand with a purposeful plan.

We can't allow brand damage to happen.

Brand Damage
It's Personal!

Larry G. Linne's Version

"Your brand cannot be *hidden*. It is created by your existence and everything you do. If you don't manage it, others may create a brand for you that isn't what you want."
—Larry G. Linne

"Proactive brand management is one of the most efficient and effective ways to maximize your success."
—Larry G. Linne

"Your personal brand is *what people think of you*. Everyone has a brand."
—Larry G. Linne

CHAPTER 1

IT STARTS AT HOME

My Kids

Most parents tell their kids they have to manage their reputations. Unfortunately, the word "reputation" has lost its impact. Kids usually translate that into "You don't want me to embarrass our family?" Unfortunately for most families, kids are too focused on themselves to be motivated by what others may think of the family. Enter social media. Now our kids' "reputation" is being communicated throughout the Internet. "What people may think" about our kids is now available at the speed of megahertz.

I have five school-age daughters. Every August I sit with each of them and ask, "At the end of this school year, what do you want your friends, classmates, and teachers to think about you?" They tell me things such as "I was nice, hardworking, inclusive of others, helpful, friendly, good at sports," and more. All my girls are unique and have different items on their lists. Then I ask them what they must do to guarantee people feel this way about them. They tell me things like: "I have to work hard, think about others first, introduce myself to new people, be prepared," and so on. Then I ask them what they have to not do, or avoid, to make sure people think these things about them. They say: "Not talk bad about others," "Not post negative things on Facebook," "Not turn in homework late," etc.

We frequently talk about personal branding and use the definition "what people think about you" in our home. Throughout the year we have discussions about how they are managing their "brands." We talk about "thinking about your brand" before posting on social media sites. We do self-checks on how we are all doing on personal brand management. It has become a fun culture for us, and our kids have really connected with the concept. I think they see brand management as a cool thing to do. It is very rewarding to hear them teaching their friends about managing their brand.

Okay, time to brag a little. My thirteen-year-old daughter had two examples during the year where she chose to not do things with kids (go to an inappropriate movie and lie about where she was going) because it would "hurt my brand." She uses the term "brand management" as a part of her normal conversation. I heard her tell one kid, "I have a bigger future and can't afford to damage my brand by doing something stupid."

My eleven-year-old daughter had a great brand management experience this past year. Her elementary school has an award for graduating fifth-grade students. The award is determined by all of the students writing an essay on another kid they believe represents the character traits the school promotes. Fortunately for my daughter, the character traits align exactly with the "brand" items she identifies at the first of the year.

The kids turn in these essays, and the teachers review the kids with the most essays written about them. Based on what is written and teacher observation from the year, the teachers vote and choose the top character student.

I asked my daughter a week before the award was announced, "How did you do in managing your brand this year?"

She said, "I think I did a good job."

Her mom and I were so proud when we went to graduation and they announced her name as the winner. This was an award based on what others *thought* about our daughter. She realized that her success was due to determining her brand, determining what she had to do and not do, and frequently thinking about and monitoring her brand throughout the year.

We make personal brand management fun in our house. We have all realized how much better our lives are when we manage what we want people to think of us. For those who think this is manipulative or out of control (family), remember everyone has a brand. Our random behaviors can send a message to others that is not true about us. Now keep in mind that we can't completely control what others think about us. Others may misinterpret our brand or what we want them to think of us. However, you have a much better chance of getting others to think certain things about you if you're purposeful rather than random.

I also believe in managing a brand that represents you. You can't hide a false brand for long. However, you can ruin a great brand with a random mistake due to a lack of awareness. Brand management is fun and gives you the ability to guide what people focus on when they think of you. This is healthy relationship management. I believe we can all have a bigger future if we manage our personal brand.

Tell Others What to Think

My second-oldest daughter is from Mongolia, China. Her name is Wen Jun. We were blessed to have her come into our family when she was thirteen years old. She has been vision impaired her entire life. She was born with only one eye and cannot see much better than 20/200 out of that eye. She is an amazing young woman and gets around incredibly well without a cane or mobility devices, though she probably should be using them 100 percent of the time. She adapts quickly to an environment and can get around as any fully sighted person does. However, she is legally blind and will never be able to see perfectly.

Many people with vision impairments are embarrassed and don't want others to know they are blind. My daughter feels this way and frequently tries to hide her blindness. It is unfortunate, because the reality is that she is amazing in how she can do so much that others can't do. When you realize she is blind, her talent and skill blow you away.

When she goes places, she never wants to use her cane. It would "brand" her as blind. She doesn't want that brand. So she goes without the cane. When she bumps into people, runs into things, or spills something—things that happen because she cannot see—people look at her with distaste. They think of her as clumsy, irresponsible, out of control, or unaware of her surroundings. They look irritated because they don't understand why she would behave in this manner. She experiences this often when she is around obnoxious kids at school who make fun of her because she is different (that is a story for another book someday).

When she has her cane, it is entirely different. She may run into someone by accident or knock something down when walking by a table. People quickly look at her with respect and smile at her. They see that she is dealing with vision impairment and realize they couldn't do what she is doing!

Watching her through this struggle has helped me to understand brand management better. I see that *we can control what others think of us in so many ways.* We can choose to let our brand just come to us, or we can tell others what to think of us. Just the use of her mobility devices can dramatically change how people perceive her. She has taught me that we have the power to tell others what to expect from us. What we wear, how we carry ourselves, and how we present ourselves are all preemptive messages about our brand.

I cannot imagine the difficulty of what my daughter must go through in battling these thoughts every day. I will never be able to completely understand. I am thankful that she has helped me learn more about brand management (and so much more) through her struggles. When I read this section to her, she was so excited. She said, "Dad, I hope others will be able to be better from my experience." Pretty cool kid.

Potential Damage

One of my daughters recently broke up with a very nice kid. She did it gracefully and made sure to try to protect his ego and confidence (as much as you can when breaking up). She immediately opened up her Facebook page on her cell phone and started to change her status to "single." I stopped her and asked, "How will that impact your brand?"

She looked at me and said, "I guess it will probably hurt his feelings and hurt his ego. So I will look like I am rubbing it in his face. I will look mean. It will cause him to post 'single' on his status, and he may say some negative things about me."

I gave her a smile and said, "Okay, and what do you want people to think about when they think of you?"

She smiled back, as we have had this kind of conversation on a regular basis. "I want people to think of me as nice and someone that treats others with respect."

"So how are you going to manage your brand on Facebook with this breakup?"

"Well, Dad, I think I could let him change his status first. Then I can make a positive statement about him on his post. Then I can change my status. Then people may see me as a nice person, and he may have a hard time saying mean things to me."

I smiled, and she knew she had nailed that one (the look on her face was priceless).

She followed through, and it played out beautifully. He posted that he was single the next day, and she immediately posted what a great guy he is and how much she enjoyed being in a relationship with him. He immediately responded back and said very positive things about my daughter. He called her classy, smart, and one of the best people he had ever known.

Over the next couple of days, many other people posted on this status change. Adults, friends of both kids, and family members all posted incredibly nice things about both of these kids. By simply asking the question "How will this impact my brand?" she was able to have a very strong brand management experience versus the potential negative one that would have been triggered by her natural instinct.

This may be the primary reason Patrick and I have found this topic to be so powerful. Our natural instincts are not the best things to follow when it comes to personal brand management. We don't have enough experience with social media in a world where information comes at us at an incredibly high speed. We are not purposeful in our brand management. We react, post, and then see what happens. Most people I know have experiences of doing something stupid on social media. These are usually items that have had a negative impact on their brand. Sometimes they are aware of it, and other times they are not.

Our posting on social media is not the only problem. Our dress, appearance, actions, social environments, and just about everything about us can be communicated by others through video (everyone has a video camera/phone in their pocket) or other forms of technology. Our brand is more public and more easily broadcast than at any other time in history. As technology increases, our personal brands will be more evident to others.

Technology is only part of the challenge. The accessibility of someone's past, present, and future sparks a desire in people to know this information. We have already seen that employers, schools, dates, and new acquaintances are frequently seeking out as much information about people as possible. This trend creates a stronger desire to access and know someone's brand either before they meet you or soon thereafter. Personal brand management is already important, but it will only become more important as we continue to evolve technology and our culture. You will see in future chapters that this increased awareness will increase the impact of our spoken words, our dress and appearance, and how we project ourselves. It is a new age. Branding has become personal.

CHAPTER 2

PERSONAL DAMAGE

Permanent Damage

I was at a board meeting for a large construction association. A new board member who I did not know was attending the session. He was introduced, and only a few people on the board had any knowledge of or relationship with him. He did a great job in the meeting. He was a great listener and did a nice job of offering the right advice at the right time. He was intelligent, had a quick wit, and was very articulate. We were all impressed and felt like we had a great new board member.

After the board meeting we had a planned dinner. We started with drinks and some appetizers in the bar area of the restaurant. This new board member went right to the hard liquor, and his personality immediately changed. He became very talkative and inappropriate. He was telling inside information about his company and colleagues. His voice became very loud, and he was embarrassing to the group (others were in the restaurant).

I could see people rolling their eyes at him and distancing themselves from him the rest of the night. He sat on the board for the next three years, and he never had as good of a day as his first board meeting. The group treated him differently from that night forward. The other board members believed he couldn't be trusted. Not one person ever became close with him. Associating with him could be very bad for one's brand. His brand was damaged in one night!

Five years later I was at a meeting in a different state. The meeting was with a group of prominent executives in the construction industry. One of them asked me if I knew the gentleman I spoke of above. I responded that I did know him. Nine of the people at this meeting started talking about him. Some told stories about him, and others expressed how they had "heard about him." All the stories were about his drinking and improper social behavior. His brand was permanently damaged. It would be very difficult for him to ever change his brand in the construction industry.

Things Are Changing

What do the following people have in common? Mark Zuckerberg, Lebron James, Jerry Sandusky, Steven Jobs, Hope Solo, and all of your employees. Every one of them has a personal brand, and every one of them has, or will have, an impact on what others think about the organization with which they are affiliated because of that brand.

Each of the names listed above gives you an emotion of some type (if you know who they are). That is what a brand does.

Hope Solo is a name that creates both positive and negative emotions, depending on your beliefs. However, it is hard to think about the US women's soccer team without thinking about Hope Solo.

You almost can't think of Penn State without Jerry Sandusky coming to mind.

Steven Jobs and Apple—certainly a natural fit.

Mark Zuckerberg is a name that can create all types of emotions about him and his style, character, youth, creativity, and more.

Okay, no big deal. This is normal, right? We have always associated big-name people with the organizations to which they belong. Ah, but has something changed?

A 2011 study of the world's top 1,000 companies (Oxford Metrica Reputation Review, 2011. Risks That Matter, OM research commissioned by Ernst & Young) identified that 832 of those companies had a minimum of a 20 percent decrease in value during the prior five-year period due to "reputation." Reputation hits were items like data breach, news about individuals in the company, product failures or recalls, political issues, or legal situations. I can't imagine any other time in history where this level of brand damage could have happened.

Lloyd's of London compiles the results of annual surveys pertaining to risk and risk preparedness. The Lloyd's Index 2011 report also revealed the changing nature of reputation and its impact on business. The CEOs identified reputation as the ninth-highest risk out of 41 different risks in 2009. The CEOs identified reputation as the third-highest risk in 2011.

Yes, times have changed. Individuals are influencing the brands of companies and will impact the value of those companies.

August 2012 Brand Survey

We sent a survey out to over ten thousand business decision makers and asked them to give us feedback on what preparation they do before meeting with a salesperson.

Seventy-eight percent of decision makers look up salespeople before meeting with them. It is very critical to understand this fact. Over three out of four decision makers are seeking out information about salespeople before they call on them. This means the brand of the salespeople precedes them. This is potentially very damaging or a great opportunity. Prior to the Internet, we had to call friends and business associates to learn about people before meeting them. This would take too long and would only happen on occasion. Now it is the norm. I ask salespeople in my numerous training classes each year if they have managed what someone would find if they were to be looked up. The majority of the people cringe and immediately begin cleaning up their online presence and starting to manage their brand. I also find the majority go look me up online within twenty-four hours. Interesting how that comes back around.

Seventy-six percent look up the company prior to meeting with a salesperson. I found this interesting, as well. Fewer people are looking up the company than looking up the person. This was surprising to us. We believed the company brand was still the primary interest. The data spoke differently, and this new reality suggests people are going to look at both when learning about a potential purchase.

Ninety-eight percent of decision makers look up details on the company that the salespeople represent after meeting with them if they are still interested in buying after the meeting. My work in sales suggests that this is a behavior of reinforcing what they saw or heard from the salesperson. The buyer is simply verifying and doing more thorough research to see if what was said aligned with what was online.

When the buyers researched people, they used the following sources:

- *Eighty-four percent used a Google search.*
- *Sixty-five percent used LinkedIn.*
- *Fifty-eight percent used Facebook.*
- *Forty-eight percent used Twitter.*
- *Fifty-four percent searched for personal Web pages.*

Social media trends will make this data obsolete relatively fast. However, we found this important to share because these entities will most likely not go away any time soon. We believe the impact of each and the order in which people use them will change over time. My Twitter account gets hit much more often than my Facebook account. The point is not to worry too much about the order; all of them can have an impact. More social media sites will come into existence and will play a role in your brand management in the future.

One of the most recent social media evolutions is on LinkedIn. They are using algorithms and pulling data from individual sites to push the people's brand out to the market. Words and phrases in a user's profile are extracted and pushed (sent to another user's page to see) to the person's connections for "endorsements." This change has created a nightmare for many people trying to manage their brand. If the endorsements come in heavy in areas they don't want to highlight, they are going to reflect a brand that is different from the desired brand. Social media will continue to use strategies that create interaction and connectivity. Proactively managing this information is a critical part of effective personal brand management.

Decision makers, on average, spend 52 percent of their research time on the person with whom they will do business and 48 percent on the company. This data suggests that, since the information is available, the buyers are spending time researching the people with whom they will do business . . . or not. People used to be able to influence what others thought about them by talking or acting in a certain way. Now our reputation is built on the past, present, and future.

Before the twenty-first century began, we were only doing word-of-mouth and phone research on companies we were considering for our business or personal purchases. When the Internet developed enough volume, we moved to more in-depth company searches and much more thorough learning about the people and companies from which we bought. Both of these methods are still being used on different levels. However, younger people are more comfortable with non-interpersonal research. The millennial generations grew up banking without going to a bank, buying music online, and sending mail electronically. It doesn't matter if word-of-mouth or online research is more effective, the shift is going to continue to move to online research. Your brand will precede you in most new relationships, like it or not.

I believe this research also shows that we have shifted the focus away from the company product or brand. Don't get me wrong, we are still looking at the company brand. However, the majority of time and energy is now being spent on the individual brands of the people in the organization. People want to know about the person as much as the company.

Patrick's Take: One individual can completely influence the brand of a company, no matter how big or small. I recently had a horrible interaction with a very large communications company. I hired the company to provide all of our Internet and phone services for SiliconCloud US based on their relatively reliable brand and the fact that I have cell and home service with them. The remote sales rep sold me service that was not available in our area, and when we finally found a package that would work, the service was never installed correctly. We canceled the order and moved to another company. Months later I received a call from a collection agency, informing me that I was delinquent on payment. The company had some errors and had left our service billing open even though we never received anything from them! While I was dealing with this and trying to get my credit restored, my family's cell bill that month was almost double what it typically was. I was at my breaking point and had had enough. I called the company to see what was going on with my cell bill and had fully intended on canceling our service and moving to another company.

The rep on the other end was extremely professional. He got right to work and showed me the reason our bill had gone up so much. He offered a quick solution and, without my asking, backdated our new plan so we would not be charged all of the overages (saving us about $150). It was by far the best customer experience I have ever had. Needless to say, we stayed with the company based on this one individual.

Yes, one person can make a difference!

This data represented businesses selling to other businesses. However, the trend is broader than business-to-business sales strategies. This data shows that it is natural and easy to find out about others and to be able to make decisions on what we think of people before we meet them. In a world where relationships have a huge impact on our ability to be successful, managing what people think of us could have a very positive impact on our personal success. I would bet that just about everyone in North America has been "looked up" by a prospective buyer, employer, friend, date, spouse, friend, kid, or someone.

In the past few months I have been to social events, church activities, and other social events during which someone has come up to me and informed me that they had looked me up on the Internet. This includes people my wife invited over to our home, neighbors, country club members, guys on my cycling team, and even the parents of the kids' soccer team. I even had one parent on a soccer team look me up on her iPad while standing next to me on the sidelines of my eight-year-old's game. She tried to be discrete, but since Patrick manages my Internet presence so well, when she typed my name in the search bar, the Google results page lit up with my name (relevant and positive information thankfully). It was hard to hide.

The personal brand train has left the station. Your brand is public and quickly accessible. Actually, some would say, "You can't find me on the Internet." Well, I would say your brand is evident, as well!

If you throw in social media, the Internet (and the speed of information traveling), and cameras on smartphones and cell phones, all of a sudden a single individual in your company has the ability to damage a company brand in a moment of poor judgment.

The wrong thing said to the wrong person. A poor customer service experience posted on YouTube. An illegal act posted on a video or on Facebook. Damaging or positively impacting a brand is now a full-time job. We will show many examples of positive and negative brand management throughout the rest of this book. You can look at the daily news and see it playing out. When we can learn of major news about people all over the world within a few hours because of Twitter, we have to accept that our brand can no longer be hidden.

Keep in mind that our new era of personal brand management is also an opportunity.

I recently had a company decide to do business with me because they were able to research my 9.5 Alive foundation. This foundation raises money to support orphans and educating women in undeveloped countries. He liked what he saw and made the decision to do business with me because of my brand, before he learned anything about my product!

Your company brand is a combination of the company and the individuals in the company. The strength of or the damage to your brand will come more often from individuals in today's business environment.

CHAPTER 3

HOW LONG DOES IT TAKE TO GET A BRAND?

Thirty Seconds

In the eleventh grade, my high school philosophy teacher told our class, "People will spend the first thirty seconds when they meet you forming an opinion about you. Then they will spend the future of their relationship with you trying to find evidence to support their initial opinions." This was probably the beginning of my desire to manage my personal brand. As I grew older and went into professional sports and sales, I spent years working on perfecting this concept. My wardrobe was mostly purchased based on how I wanted people to initially think of me. I practiced my thirty-second commercials, worked on voice quality, and made certain it matched that of a trusted adviser in strength, confidence, and tone. Bottom line, I wanted to manage what people thought of me in the beginning of our relationship. This would allow people to focus on my products, intellectual property, or advice, as opposed to attributes that distracted from my sales proposition. Managing what people think about me in that first impression has worked very well for me (not that I have always done it perfectly).

What people think of you will influence decisions to buy from you, spend time with you, work for or with you, listen to you, or even have a relationship with you. Managing the first thirty seconds of a relationship is one of the most powerful brand management strategies in existence.

It is an unfortunate reality though. I can't imagine that everyone is correct in his or her thirty-second evaluation of someone. So we had a real challenge to makes sure we were lucky enough to influence people the way we wanted to in those first thirty seconds.

Four Minutes

In July 2008 my wife invited a new friend and her husband over for dinner. I had not met them prior to this dinner, so I figured the evening would be more interesting if I did a little research on them before they arrived. I searched Google and Ask.com, and I found articles, work history, and various other bits of information about each of them within about four minutes of research. Prior to their arrival, I was so proud and impressed with how good I was going to be in conversations. I was bragging to my wife about how I was going to be crafty with my questions and conversations topics.

The couple arrived, and we began to get to know each other. I was thinking about how I would begin to introduce conversations based on my research. When the guy said, "Larry, I was looking you up online this afternoon, and I was impressed with what I saw."

Now what would I do? My game was ruined. I couldn't dance around the fact that I had looked him up, as well. I had to fess up.

"That is so funny," I responded. "I looked you up today, as well. I saw you caught a big tarpon." That's all I had. My brilliant strategy turned into a simple, dumb statement. However, that moment became the beginning of a new realization in personal brand management. People will spend about four minutes learning about you via your Internet footprint prior to meeting you!

In the years following this dinner, researching and predetermining thought development have clearly become the norm. This is especially true with business relationships. Since this event, I have been told many times that I have been "looked up." Regarding this "minus four minutes," it is important to recognize that your brand precedes your physical presence. Your footprint on the Internet will include pictures, videos, articles about you, articles or blogs you have written, social media content, and comments others may have made about you. Some of you think, *Ha! This doesn't apply to me. You can't find anything about me on the Internet.*

First, it is easy to find information about people online. It doesn't take much effort to find the price of a house, someone's estimated income, a social security number, a driver's license number, credit history, marriage information, an address, and much more. Second, if people's presence is limited online, they will be considered "old school" and not up to speed with what the world is doing. That was okay in a world where it took a full generation to evolve how we interacted or did business. But in a world that changes daily, if someone wants to be considered relevant, it is important to manage a brand online and off.

We will address how to maximize your footprint in a later chapter. However, it is critical to manage your "minus four minutes."

Two Years: The Opportunity!

Patrick has continually hounded me to write blogs, do vlogs, write articles, and connect with others in the same media. He set up my website and our company websites. He has connected our entire online footprint to maximize control of what people find when they look us up.

I have worked extensively in the insurance industry over the past few years. That industry is not cutting edge when it comes to technology and Internet usage. It is currently the summer of 2012 (with the speed of technological change, that is relevant). One day, a couple of weeks ago, I had multiple conversations about doing business with two different CEOs of insurance agencies in the United States. One of these CEOs was in South Carolina, and the other was in Minnesota. In both discussions they informed me that it was not necessary to give any introduction or background on myself because they had already been reading my articles, blogs, and websites, along with my LinkedIn page and other information, for the past two years. My brand was established as a trusted and respected consultant/ adviser two years prior to the calls. They were already looking for advice and my intellectual property when we started the call. This new opportunity of proactive brand management is speeding up the sales process, changing the sales process, and creating opportunities that didn't exist before.

If you are required to interact with others in your career, it is going to help the level of success if a positive brand precedes them.

Most people in the professional sales arena have a huge hurdle to jump when it comes to being trusted and perceived as credible. They have to spend time early in their sales process creating credibility and a brand that gives the perception that they should be heard and believed, and that they are capable. What if they didn't have to do that? What if their brand preceded them? What if buyers believed they were credible long before they arrived? How would that change how they sell? How would that impact the speed of selling? The answers to these questions are being seen in the positive results from salespeople who are proactively managing their brand. Many salespeople that I coach are walking in as true trusted advisers, because the buyer already sees them as credible and worthy. It changes everything in the sales process.

Patrick's Take: Brand management isn't reserved for seasoned sales veterans alone. The differentiation and proactive messaging described above can be implemented by young, inexperienced people, as well.

Larry and I used to run classes that taught young salespeople how to become true professionals. One of the main hurdles that most of these rookies faced was creating perceived value. We would teach them different strategies to combat the reality of their youth. One of these was to fully embrace technology. If they were willing to purposefully manage their brand, provide valuable content (e.g., blogs and other commentary on market issues), and utilize technology to connect, then they had a distinct advantage over some of the seasoned professionals in their market sector.

If our rookies had a purposefully managed brand and their competitor did not, they would go into a prospect meeting with a leg up right off the bat! As we know, their prospect was most likely going to search for them online prior to the meeting. If our rookies' search results came back positive and powerful, and their competitor was old, outdated, or even nonexistent, this was certainly beneficial for them. These differentiation strategies don't apply just online.

One of the most powerful and effective stories of offline brand management that we ever encountered was that of a young insurance producer in Florida. This producer fully understood the power of personal branding and the idea of "birds of a feather flocking together" (which we will address later in the book). He knew he didn't have years of experience and results to sell, so he looked for another way to get noticed by decision makers.

This young producer was only a few years out of college and was still a huge supporter of his school's football team. He donated enough money to be at the top level of the university's booster club (something he saw as an investment in himself, more than a donation or expense), which allowed him access to the luxury suites at games. Instead of tailgating and hanging out with his buddies, this producer made a bold move by becoming the youngest member of the elite level inside the booster club. Just as Larry created positive buzz with his online branding, this young producer did the same with his involvement in the booster club. Yes, his reputation preceded him, and it was very positive.

The opportunity we have today is to manage our brands with years of information prior to meeting someone. The game has changed. The proactive management of information about individuals is a critical strategy for anyone who depends on new relationships for their success.

CHAPTER 4

BRAND CREATION

My Brand

Since brands change so fast, I can tell you things about my brand today. By the time you read this, many items will have evolved. However, I believe your understanding of my brand and how I manage it will give you clarity on many of these points.

I have fun at many of my events and ask the audience to tell me what they think of me. I ask them to write down what they think of me on a piece of paper. I have my desired brand written on my iPad. I look at my brand daily so I can make sure to manage it. When they are finished writing things down, I ask them to tell me what they think of me. It is always rewarding when they tell me exactly what is on my paper. They are amazed at how I do this. Some feel like it is magic or something. I know exactly why they think certain things. I either told them to think it, or I purposefully did something that would influence their thinking.

I am going to ask you to not judge me negatively by this section. It is not easy to put these items in a book (and be pretty transparent) and express to the world what I want you to think about me. However, I am doing this to help you with your brand. So I hope my intentions are well received.

Some items on my desired brand list include: intelligent, thought leader, disciplined, healthy and fit, and adoration for my family. How do I influence others to have these thoughts?

Intelligent. I reference other smart people frequently. I read a lot and refer to these books when teaching, speaking, and interacting with others. I read highly complex books and express opinions about those books.

Thought leader. I write blogs about current events and make arguments that are new and challenging to my readers. My desire is to open new files in the minds of my audience every time I write, speak, or interact with others. I persuade versus inform.

Disciplined. This is shown mostly through my eating, lack of drinking in public, and health. People know me to be fit and strong. As a blockheaded German, it doesn't take much to convince people that I am naturally disciplined.

Healthy and fit. This one is relatively easy to manage. Just be healthy and fit. However, I post items on my social media to highlight bike racing, workouts, and other health-related activities to let people know my level of seriousness regarding being fit.

Adoration for my wife and five daughters. I use social media for this area of brand management. With a big public image comes being unapproachable at times. So it is important that I make myself real to others and allow them to see what I value the most.

These are things I do to get people to believe certain things about me. However, I have to do other things to protect my brand. I use much of my social media space to communicate the softer and approachable side of my personality. I constantly evaluate my clothes and how I dress for different events and activities. I use the model of "half up" in my dress. Whatever the recommended dress is for an event, I go half up. An example would be wearing long dress slacks to play golf. I may wear a jacket over a dress shirt at a business casual event. You can usually just add a piece of clothing (or add length to clothing) to be half up. I find that the person dressed a little nicer usually represents someone in charge or in more of an advisory-level position. They tend to be respected a bit more and get recognized. Now be careful: dressing a full level up can put you out of place and give a brand image of inappropriate and showing off.

Patrick looks at my Internet presence daily to make sure others aren't damaging my brand and to make sure I haven't done something stupid. Our family watches out for each other and makes sure we are projecting a proper family brand.

Brand management is full-time work. When you get it down, it becomes second nature and part of your everyday activities. It is comforting. When someone is misunderstood, it can be very frustrating. Proper brand management increases the chance of being understood exactly the way you desire. Please understand, you won't guarantee your brand, but once again it is much better than letting your brand happen by chance.

My Team

My adviser team is the strongest in the insurance and risk consulting business. They are experienced, intelligent, and intuitive, and they get results for their clients. I have learned a lot about personal branding from working with this team.

Every few months I ask them, "What do you want people to think of when they think of you?" They have a few core things that never change. Some have brands that represent their actual experience in the insurance business. Some have brands of being outstanding teachers. Our Canadian adviser is known for being excellent in operations management. One of the advisers has a fantastic brand around hiring and HR evaluations.

However, they have to constantly evolve their brand around items that will improve the impact they can make on others. One of my advisers has been including more examples of his studying and reading when he gives speeches. This is to create a stronger brand of his intelligence and knowledge. Another adviser has great sales skills but wants people to see him as credible in leadership principles. He makes sure to open discussions with clients in the areas that are more leadership—and operations-focused. This allows him the opportunity to create a brand in this area.

The lessons I have with this team is how frequent we need to address our brand. Personal brand management is not natural, and it isn't easy. They find it hard to define the brand and how they will impact that brand. One way I have influenced them to control their brand is to prepare them for events. If we have a meeting with clients, prior to the event they are required to articulate (to me) how they will influence what people think of them.

They are becoming very talented at identifying and managing their brands. They think through it and come up with great strategies. When we have these discussions we are always shocked at how purposeful we have to be to make sure we get people to think what we want them to think about us. They all have tendencies to go to things that actually damage their brands. But when we work through this process, they are very purposeful and skilled at making a strong impact with their brand.

One of my team members is a female adviser. She has a very strong background in operations and smaller business sales. She is known in Canada as one of the most experienced and knowledgeable advisers in these areas.

Fast-forward twenty years. This woman has worked hard over the past twenty years and has expanded her skills and knowledge in many new areas. She has developed skills in leadership, finance, sales, and CEO-level advising. As a matter of fact, she is one of the people I go to for advice on a lot of issues now. She has a huge problem with getting people to allow her to give advice in these areas. They want to go straight to operations issues when they are around her. It is very frustrating to her because she has so much more to offer. She couldn't break this brand issue, because every time anyone would come up to her at a meeting or event, they would start the conversation around operations or small business items. She would be caught in the conversation, enhancing that brand.

We started working on her brand. We developed some new strategies:

1. Have conversation starters that are not associated with operations and small business. Be prepared to bring up these conversations when you start a conversation.
2. Start conversations versus letting others start them.
3. Speak on topics related to the new brand versus the old brand items.
4. Blog and write about the new items.

Over a two-year period she moved her brand closer to these desired items. It worked very well. Her next challenge was her internal team (the other advisers). They continued to feed her all the operations consulting work, and they were sending a brand message that she is "the operations person." So she and I communicated her desired brand to them. We gave them examples of her strengths and unique knowledge in many areas of leadership, finance, sales, and CEO-level management. We proactively managed how they would influence her brand, as well, by giving them new ways to deal with the operations items versus sending them to her.

This was a great lesson for me: realizing that we can proactively manage our brand by identifying what we want people to think and purposefully manage the key touch points with those we want to influence. But we may have to have others help us, as well. Our family, friends, and colleagues have an influence on our brand. We need to give them clarity about our brand so they don't damage it. I have had great success in letting others know my desired brand. It not only helps me by their supporting that brand but also helps me be accountable to deliver on that brand.

So being purposeful and having continual management of your brand are critical to the overall management of your brand. Don't let others own it. You own it, and you have to manage it, or your brand will not be what you want it to be.

Steps to a Great Brand

Brand creation and management need to be purposeful and consistent. It is not a one-time event, and it will evolve throughout your life. The following steps are one way to develop and manage your brand. Patrick will be introducing another model in his section. Don't get too caught up in what is the right way to do this. As long as you are doing something, you will be ahead of the majority of people in the world.

Step 1: Write down what you believe people think of you today. Make sure to write all the positive, negative, and neutral items that come to mind. Ask others to give you information, as well. However, be careful. They may not tell you everything you need to know. You will clearly get the positive things. The negative things will be the hardest to extract. If you have very close friends, ask them to be brutally honest and let you know what others think of you. If you have the ability to get anonymous feedback from people in your work environment, it is helpful.

Examples: Hardworking, disciplined, intelligent, calm, caring, philanthropic, hardheaded, tough, approachable, and high risk.

Step 2: Think about your future. Write down your goals, and describe your ideal future. Write down what characteristics you want to have to maximize your potential of reaching your ideal future. Do you need to be perceived as intelligent? Would it benefit you to be thought of as honest or hardworking? Are you a problem solver or researcher? Are you detailed, focused, and kind? Think about what attributes and characteristics would benefit you the most to reach your ideal future.

Example: Intelligent, problem solver, creative, innovative, honest, disciplined, detailed, focused, results-oriented, etc.

Step 3: Do a gap analysis. What is the difference between your brand today and your desired brand? This is the hard part. Your objective here is to get clarity on what needs to be changed or developed to reach your desired brand. Simply list what is the same and what is different.

Example: Items that are on the second list but not the first: problem solver, creative, innovative, honest, detailed, focused, and results-oriented.

Step 4: Develop action items to build a new brand (or break old brand items).

Example: Innovative—start bringing some ideas to meetings, and be prepared to sell those ideas. Don't be protective of new innovations and ideas. Let people know what I am thinking. Let people know I research new ideas and am very creative.

Step 5: Identify where and how you will project your brand. Realize that dress, style, what you drive, voice tone and quality, friends, recreation, weight, health, social environments, religious affiliations, where you live, language you use, what you reference in conversations, and social media postings all have an influence on your brand. Think about what conversations you need to have to manipulate what people will think of when they think of you. Become purposeful about what you post on social media and when you post it, and always ask, "How will this impact my brand?"

Example: Innovative—get in front of leaders and managers with my new ideas more often. Also, share new ideas with clients to get their feedback and input on the value of those ideas. Make sure to package my ideas to present them as high value.

Step 6: List what you must do to protect your brand. This may be one of the most critical steps. I have seen people blow their brand because of not thinking through this. Should you never drink in public? Should you not talk publicly (or not too much) about a certain area of your life? Should you always dress a certain way to get people to think a certain way about you? Make sure to identify any way your brand could be damaged, and put rules and systems in place to protect your brand.

Example: Innovative—don't show innovative ideas without thinking through them and having confidence they will work. Poor ideas that are not well thought out will damage my brand as being innovative.

Step 7: Rinse and repeat. Every six months you need to go back through steps one through six. Your brand will change and evolve. Stay on it.

Don't get too caught up in details and let this bog you down. The keys are to identify what you want your brand to be and act accordingly. These details will help you refine and perfect your brand. Bottom line: do something to be proactive in brand identification and management. It will help!

African Children Use Branding to Influence Community

Milton Opoya is from a rural community in Uganda, Africa. He grew up in poverty, but his parents sacrificed everything, including their house, to ensure he went to school. Selling their house left the family homeless, and they were forced to live under a tree. He ended up attending university and eventually graduated. Through all of this, Milton never forgot the sacrifice of his parents.

Kampala is a community in Uganda that has areas of extreme poverty. As with any region with this level of poverty, there are not only economic issues but also social issues. One of the major problems facing this area is street kids. Unfortunately, many young boys end up living on the street due to cases of abuse and their parents' death. Some families do not have enough room or resources to care for the entire family. Girls are seen as income generators due to dowries, and boys are seen as revenue drains. These children are forgotten because no one wants them. In order to survive, these children turn to stealing and other deviant behaviors. Many times they turn to drugs simply to curb the feeling of hunger. There is no future for them.

In 2007, Milton was working as a bookkeeper for a nonprofit organization. He quickly realized that his true passion was to engage the forgotten children and do something bigger than accounting functions. In 2008, Milton and his wife rented a home and went out to the slums of Kampala to start connecting with the homeless children. He soon found five boys that expressed their desire for a better life. African Child in Need was started. Currently ACN cares for twenty-three boys. They provide clothing, shelter, basic health care, and education for the boys. Milton is doing this because of the sacrifice his parents made for him, and he is trying to give a voice to the voiceless and hope to the hopeless children of Uganda.

Along with the obvious struggles that these children face, there is another situation that has arisen. Because of their past as street kids, this children have a horrible reputation as thieves and bad people. The neighbors around Milton's home do not want these children in the area. They do not hide this. They verbally assault the children as they come and leave, and there are high levels of tension. The boys are seen as very dangerous.

Enter Michael Loeters. Michael is one of our clients. For the past few years, Michael has traveled to Africa during his summer holiday in order to give to those in need. He became aware of Milton and African Child in Need and began working with them. Michael has gone through several branding exercises and conversations with us. He fully understands the importance of personal branding, and he saw a huge opportunity to bring this concept to Kampala.

On his last trip, Michael decided to take some of our concepts and ran two separate personal branding workshops. The first was with the boys to help them manage their brand, and the second was with Milton. He discussed the concepts:

- You have a brand.
- What is a brand?
- What are you doing to reinforce your current brand?
- Identify your future brand.
- You have the power to change your brand over time.

The boys in the home range in age from eight to eighteen years old. Even with their strained background, they are still typical young boys. They try to act macho around their friends. They are very into the urban/hip-hop culture, which influences their speech, dress, dance, and attitude. Sometimes they lash out at the neighbors in retaliation for their verbal abuse, and they are typically treated extremely poorly at school. Frequently, teachers call them thieves and tell them that they are worthless. They are all good boys, but this image that they are portraying is sadly reinforcing the negative stereotype that their neighbors, teachers, and others put on them.

During his workshop with them, Michael tried to help them understand how their actions, words, dress, etc., affect what people think of them. At first, this wasn't having the planned effect. The kids were just blowing it off as another message of growing up or not acting like they felt they needed to act to be cool. He then began discussing what they liked and who they listened to on the radio. Unanimously they answered Lil Wayne. Lil Wayne is an American rap artist. Michael then began asking the boys what they thought of Lil Wayne as a person, not an artist. Again they unanimously answered, "He's a criminal." (We are not representing that this is true about Lil Wayne. It is simply what the kids said.) They said this because of his lyrics, his dress, and the things they heard about him. *Ding!* The lightbulb went off. They quickly understood that their emulating him and others was how people thought of them. Their reputation was being communicated loud and clear, and they weren't happy with the message they were sending.

The second workshop was a one-on-one with Milton. Michael went over the issues that he discussed with the boys and the importance of Milton's role in reinforcing these concepts to manage their reputations.

He is the brand manager. Next, Michael turned his focus to Milton. As Milton has said, African Child in Need gives a voice to the voiceless and hope to the hopeless. This is very true and positive; however, they needed to work on a more powerful message. Milton regularly has to meet with the boys' teachers, the neighbors, other street boys, and community members. It is often hard for him to communicate the importance of his organization's work. Michael and Milton worked hard and got to the root of what ACN truly does. They are developing the future leaders of Uganda. These boys are taken in and given a chance to develop into family figureheads, community leaders, and leaders of the country. That is a powerful message and shows the potential impact of ACN on the country as a whole.

Michael and Milton worked through a plan to continue to manage the boys' brand, how that ties to ACN, and how ACN can help enhance that reputation.

Many of the boys are having a different impact on the community now that they are managing their brand. They see themselves from a perspective of those who are looking at them versus from their own internal view of themselves. It will take time for the community to completely change their view of these boys. But progress has already been made, and more progress seems to be clearly in the future. They are no longer managing the brand of the center or the boys by chance. It is a proactive brand management strategy, and it is working.

A recent success has shown the boys how powerful personal brand management can be. One of the fifteen-year-old boys has real creative talent. He makes jewelry from beads and loves the fashion scene. By changing his personal brand he was able to get acceptance in the fashion community in Kampala, eventually getting models to wear his jewelry during shows. He has started an online store, selling his jewelry, and is gaining recognition for his creative talents. He has gone from being a street kid to a recognized and respected designer in the Ugandan fashion community. He was only able to get this opportunity by changing his brand. The door was opened when they were willing to accept him.

After returning from Uganda, Michael posted the picture (Exhibit A) of him running the branding workshop with the boys. Unsolicited, Milton wrote, "This workshop changed my life!!!!!"

Milton is still reinforcing these concepts with his boys, and he is helping them manage their brand. He plans on using this with his new center that he is opening for troubled girls.

CHAPTER 5

BUZZ LIGHTYEAR

A Brand Can Make a Difference

Nick Rait was one of the most positive people ever to walk this earth. At the age of sixteen he was diagnosed with cancer. He ended up beating it twice and finally lost the battle the third time. He was nineteen years old when he passed away.

Patrick and I came to know of Nick and learn his absolutely inspirational story shortly before he passed. During the three and a half years that Nick went through treatments, got better and then much worse, and was cancer-free, he always remained positive. Experiencing being a cancer survivor twice and knowing the importance of cancer research in children, Nick started a nonprofit called Wacky Warriors. The concept is for people doing races, such as bike races, marathons, triathlons, and 5K fun runs, to dress up wackily and raise money for survivors and research. Nick wanted to do something for others who were in the same situation as him. He wanted to make a difference by helping young people manage the challenges of cancer. Thousands of people have had the desire to help, just like Nick. Unfortunately, it can be difficult to get the message out and make a difference. A lot of charities and programs compete for donors and supporters of these types of programs. However, Nick found a way to create a strong brand that made a big difference and continues to make a difference after he has left us.

While in treatment, Nick would dress up at the hospital to keep things light. He would wear funny wigs, and he even dressed as Buzz Lightyear for a marathon. He was too sick at that point, so he sprinted and beat everyone the first ten meters, and then he pulled off the raceway. A video of Nick in his Buzz Lightyear outfit is on the Wacky Warriors website at www.wackywarriors.org.

Nick had created a brand of being fun, having a positive focus, and having gratitude for everything in life. This brand generated a tremendous following for his charity.

Patrick and I learned about Wacky and what Nick and his family were doing, and it truly inspired us. Nick had a "never quit, total positivity, make the most out of life, and inspire others" mentality. There are thousands of nonprofits out there, but Nick and his brand were extremely positive and powerful, and that made us want to get involved. His passions are exuded in the Wacky guidelines:

1. Pay it forward through service to others.
2. Always have something exciting to look forward to.
3. Have fun!

I was so motivated by Nick and Wacky's cause that I decided to race for Wacky Warriors. I trained diligently for months to get ready for the Leadville 100, which is the toughest mountain bike race in the United States. I set a goal and began raising money and awareness for Wacky Warriors. Three weeks prior to the race I had a bad training accident. I hit a rock with my pedal, which sent me over the handlebars and straight down onto the trail. This left me with a separated shoulder, torn ligaments, and broken bones in my arm and hand. Patrick called to check on me that day, and we spoke as I was leaving the hospital. He asked if my injuries were going to put me out of the race. My reply was "Oh, hell no. I've come too far, and I'm doing this for Nick."

Within two days I was back on the bike preparing and training for Leadville. I ended up not only competing in the race but also completing it. It was insane to do, but I had to do it. Even with all of those injuries, the Wacky Samurai (my wacky costume) fought through the pain, exhaustion, and elements to cross the finish line. I had a picture of Nick pinned on my glove. I knew that nothing would have stopped Nick if he had the opportunity to race. That kept me going.

With all of that said, I never met Nick. Nick had planned on making it out to Colorado to see me race, but his fight with cancer ended before the Leadville 100 race.

Nick's brand was so powerful that his determination, positive attitude, gratitude, and drive inspired me and continues to inspire others to push themselves to the limits while helping a great cause. Nick may not have known just how powerful his message was or how clear his brand was being received, but I am certain that it has forever changed the people who knew him and know his story.

A brand can reach further than your presence. Prior to the Internet, a brand reached only as far as the physical presence of the individual and the immediate relationships where they interact. The Internet has expanded a person's brand to become accessible to anyone who desires to find it. Access to information allows for a brand to reach a long way, very fast. Nick created a brand that influenced others. His brand made a difference, and it still is thriving beyond his life. Nick was just a normal kid living a normal life. When he realized he had an opportunity to have greater purpose, it was through a brand that he was able to create a bigger personal platform. His brand is continuing beyond his life. People continue to dress in wacky clothes for races all over the country.

CHAPTER 6

OFFENSE

Age of the Big Offense

The NFL has had major changes in the last ten years. The New England Patriots, Denver Broncos, Green Bay Packers, San Francisco 49ers, and Washington Redskins were all big offense teams that made it to the play-offs. Big offenses have taken over the game and are dominating in on-field and off-field performance (i.e., money). It is the age of the big offense. They said the offense wins games but defense wins Super Bowls. That was true for over forty years. However, the past six Super Bowls have proven the power of a big offense.

As an ex-NFL offensive player, I see an offense as something that is taking initiative and pushing toward results. A great offense can make changes based on the conditions that change around it. The key is to find the competitive advantage and exploit it! This new NFL style is risky, aggressive, and bold, and it uses multiple resources and stays ahead of the competition (and most defenses).

These are the same strategies we should be using to manage our personal brand. Technology, social network development and activity, push/pull strategies, Internet strategies, strategic physical attendance, and continued change to the conditions around us are critical to a successful brand.

I hesitate to spell out the details of how to execute an offensive strategy. Things are changing very fast. Whatever I communicate that needs to be done today will probably be obsolete in a few months. So keep in mind the concepts more than the details of the strategy.

Tim Tebow stepped into the Broncos' starting offense in 2011. He had a great run for six games and startled the world with a "different" offense. By the time he played the New England Patriots, he was considered a potential Pro Bowl candidate. Unfortunately for him (and Bronco fans), Tim ran into a coach who had figured out that offensive scheme and destroyed it. Then every team after that figured him out and shut him down. Game over. The need for reinvention had to begin.

The same thing is happening with personal brand management. What I am doing today to manage my brand with blogs, video blogs, videos, Twitter, Facebook, LinkedIn, voice and screen capture software, V-mail, and public appearances could be worthless and dead a year from now. We have to be aggressive with what is available to communicate our brand. We also have to be aware of trends and buyer behaviors to not get left behind.

Patrick's Take: First, I'd like to comment on Tim Tebow. For many years, I lived in Jacksonville Beach, Florida, which is about an hour and a half from the home of the University of Florida Gators. I've been a huge fan of the Gators since moving to Jacksonville back in 2000. It was impossible (not nearly impossible, but absolutely impossible) to escape the phenomenon that was Tebow mania during his time as quarterback for the Gators. Tebow was certainly a talented college quarterback, but maybe more importantly he was a brand! Love him or hate him (usually opposing school fans), you would certainly have a very clear and powerful opinion of Tebow.

He was, and is, extremely purposeful about his brand. He's intelligent, hardworking, disciplined, and unshakable in his ethics and faith. Regardless of your view of him on the field, it is hard to not like him. He is certainly someone who I hope my son would want to emulate when he is older. During his rookie season in the NFL he was considered one of the most recognizable figures in all of sports! His signature prayer moments seen on the sidelines went viral. People all over the social media world posted pictures of themselves "Tebowing." I'd say that his brand had an impact on people.

As for being aggressive with your brand, I couldn't agree more. We often take many of the current luxuries in life for granted. When you really think back to how much life has changed in the last eight years, it's scary. Eight years ago there was no iPhone, Droid, or personal tablets, and most of us used our cell phones for phone calls only. Facebook and Twitter weren't invented, and digital marketing was still in its infancy (it still is). When you look at all that has changed in this short amount of time, you have to realize that the way you manage your brand today will certainly change. I encourage clients to be right on the leading edge when it comes to technology. I would never tell them to jump into every single "next big thing"; however, we look at all that's out there and make decisions based on their brand.

For example, in July 2011, when we began writing this book, we looked at all the technologies and social media to ensure that we covered the bases. Now, it is winter 2012, and Pinterest has taken the United States by storm, and MySpace (remember that?) has reemerged from the rubble. The point is that things are changing at lightning speed, and you need to be aware of these changes to ensure that you are managing your brand in the appropriate channels.

In 2000, I was a member of two country clubs, because a large number of my clients and prospects were members of those clubs. I wanted to hang out where my clients were hanging out. Today I hang out on social media and in the cyber world. I could get to three to five people per week at the country club. With big events a few times a year, I could get to forty to fifty of them in a week. Today I can reach hundreds of clients and prospects a day inside of my social communities. Numerous times in 2012 I have reached thousands with a single message.

You have the potential to develop a very large "cyber country club." Creating purposeful social media accounts, blogging, connecting with others who write blogs, commenting on others' articles and white papers, and being active in your social media will give you a group of people that can be your country club audience. It is not our purpose in this book to do specific social media training. Many very good specialists in this area are keeping up with the daily changes and trends for social media maximization. Patrick does a great job of it, as well. However, this book is way too stagnant to be able to give you the specific plans and tools. The one thing that can be taught in the stagnant book is that creating a network of connections, and managing that network as a distribution system for whatever you want to sell or give to them, is critical if you want to maximize your future earnings potential.

Okay, I have put you off too long on this offensive strategy. Please forgive me if this is an "old" offense at the time you are reading this book.

Just keep in mind that you must be aware of the latest strategies and be at the current "country club" that is available to you.

Current Offense

- Quarterly review of what I want people to think of me. I have mentioned numerous times that your brand is what people think of you. A desired brand is what you want people to think of you. I find it critical to visit my brand every ninety days. This is because things change fast and new habits can form. Determining what I desire others to think of me is the first step to getting them to think it. This quarterly exercise gives me new clarity and helps me keep it top of mind.

- Annual feedback from friends, business associates, and family on what they think about me (my brand). My friends and coworkers have learned how powerful proactive brand management can be. So we frequently give each other feedback on our brands. I ask people throughout my workplace what they think and what they believe my brand is to others. It is a great exercise, because I learn a lot. The best advice I can give you here is to always say thank you for advice. Never question it, challenge it, or disagree with it. If you do, you will never get honest feedback again. Just say thank you, and deal with it as a perception (positive or negative).

- What I wear, what I drive, and how I act are decided upon. These items impact my brand, and therefore I am purposeful about each of them. I actually dress way down locally because I don't do business in my town. Therefore, I want my personal brand to be different from my business brand.

- Video blogs on the front of two websites: a personal and a company website. Keeping active in as many places as possible gives me a broader reach with my brand. Frequent video updates on my sites keep people coming back to watch what I have to say. It also helps get my name at the top of the list in a Google search.

- Written blogs on the front of two websites: a personal and a company website. Keeping fresh and making sure my blog messages support my brand is necessary and valuable. My wife has a couple of blogs, and people love reading her work. You don't have to be a published author to have something to say and share with others. Learn to blog, have fun giving others ideas and thoughts, and package them in ways to create interest and challenge. It will give you a great brand.

- Guest blog for other influential websites. I write blogs for a few different organizations. People are looking for content. If you can write something with good content, reach out and offer to write something for an organization that can help your brand.

- Twitter account to push articles, thoughts, intellectual capital, and brand messages. This is the key strategy to expand my network. Twitter allows you to push articles and ideas to your network. If the content is high quality, your connections will re-Tweet those messages. When new people see quality content, they will connect with you. This is the method that allows you to expand your network quickly. I had less than a hundred friends on LinkedIn for six years. I had over a thousand friends in six months when I used my Twitter and LinkedIn combination push strategy.

- LinkedIn page to be found by business relationships. It is also an offensive strategy to see who is looking me up and to reach out to first- and second-level relationships. This is by far the most powerful and effective way to expand your professional reach. After all, that is why it was created in the first place.

- Personal Facebook account to push my "human" brand. As an author, speaker, and industry thought leader, I am seen as untouchable at times. I connect with people on Facebook to show that I have a family and do normal things like ride bikes, work out, etc. Some people say, "I don't want to share my personal information out there on Facebook. I don't think other people care what I am doing." I find that interesting that those people would tell the people at their country club that information in the past!

You have to put it in perspective. I believe it is valuable to share your personal side with people. We can connect on such a deeper level with people if they know us as a father, husband, friend, coach, etc. Facebook allows us to be real people and share that with others. I love how I can connect with over half of my clients on the personal side of their lives through Facebook. Knowing we have kids, spouses, and life challenges can bring great value to our relationships. We can be misunderstood a lot in our lives, but Facebook helps people see the deeper purpose of my life, and it provides others with a clear picture of why I do all the things I do in my life.

- Business Facebook page for communicating updates to my products and latest business ideas. This page is the least active of all my offensive strategies. However, I consider it critical because it is another measure of success (number of "Likes"). Facebook creates opportunity for buzz and talk about my businesses. It is another world of connectivity. Creating connection groups that are interested in my work has great benefit. People frequently comment to me about my posts and thought leadership. I make sure to post thoughts and comments on the site on a regular basis. I don't do it too often or people will think I don't have anything else to do but post on my Facebook page (that would be a negative brand). Good-quality content that makes people think or inspires them is what I want on my company Facebook page.
- Attend key industry and business events as a speaker. This strategy allows me to tell people what to think of me. I get frequent requests to speak at events all over the world. Not everyone will get these kinds of opportunities. However, if you can learn to speak well, the opportunities are endless. Local clubs, schools, businesses, and all kinds of events are looking for emcees, speakers, teachers, and those who can present and entertain. This could be a good strategy to include in one's brand.

Managing your brand by protecting or waiting for others to figure out your brand will guarantee you have a brand you don't want. Be aggressive, and find the media outlets to get your brand in front of the right people. You may make some mistakes in this strategy. Tom Brady (quarterback of the New England Patriots) has thrown interceptions. However, he comes back and throws a few touchdown passes, and the interception is forgotten. If you are aggressive with your brand, you can overcome a lot of mistakes with the right media at the right time.

Just keep in mind what we taught in the early part of this book. Before you do anything, make sure to ask yourself, "How will this activity impact how others think of me?"

CHAPTER 7

BRANDING ISN'T THAT COMPLEX

Many people are beginning to realize they have to build a brand. They see it as a daunting task and usually start calling branding companies to help them with their brand. Branding can be very difficult, and I believe some elements of help and support are valuable. Some of the marketing and branding companies I have worked with in the past are really valuable and do a great job. But I must warn you that many of them don't align with what you really need. This chapter is meant to help you with your thinking pertaining to marketing and branding companies.

I received a phone call from a colleague a few months ago asking for my help with a client. She said her client was getting ready to spend $140,000 on branding. This was a business doing $5 million in annual revenue. She told me she had convinced them to have a conversation with me if I would be willing to take the call.

I knew exactly what they were going to tell me on the call. They had been given a proposal from a marketing company to do massive research. They were going to survey clients, prospects, employees, and their own leadership about what they thought about them as a company. Then they would develop a brand based on what they were doing that brought great perceived and differentiated value. Here is the fun part. The final step was how they were going to create collateral material and media strategies for the business to promote the new brand.

I listened to the proposal and started firing off questions. It was clear that the company was going to base the new brand on the past and history of the company. I told the marketing company that I could write down five words/phrases on a piece of paper, and they would be exactly what they would learn about my client in that research (which would cost them over $25,000). They said they didn't believe I could. So I asked them to make a deal with me. I wrote down these words/phrases: trustworthy, involved in the community, knows insurance, well connected, and good reputation (what most insurance agencies' feedback would include). I showed this list to them and said, "If what you find is the same as my list, will you give the $25,000 back to the client and pay me $25,000?" They said, "No. How about if we do a small sampling to verify what you think and then we can work on the present and future pieces with you?"

I liked that strategy much better. It was a $3,500 solution. I encourage you to think long and hard before you let marketing companies spend your money, telling you what you already know. The client worked with the marketing firm to do the things where they could get true value from the relationship.

I struggle with how businesses continue to let this model stay alive in modern business. Marketing and branding companies want you to believe you don't know anything about your clients, prospects, who you are, or who you want to be. They use a lot of marketing jargon to make you feel like you are not smart enough to figure these things out. So they charge you huge amounts of money to end up telling you what you already know. Only a few times have I seen marketing research provide great value to the buyer. But this is rare. Usually they are able to tell you what you already know. The worst part of this model is that they are designing a brand based solely on the past. Your brand needs to be focused on what you want people to think about you, not what they have thought of you.

I had a very successful marketing company in my early years of business. It was designed around showing businesses that they had the data and information required to do their own marketing. I taught them how to do their own marketing research, planning, and execution. The clients were amazed at how easy it was for them to understand the data and to be able to determine what they wanted people to think of them. They also knew how they could get clients to have those desired thoughts. We would hire marketing companies to help in the execution, but we would save them 50 to 60 percent of the marketing company's fees and have a stronger brand and process by doing the work themselves.

Now before I get a bunch of phone calls from marketing companies, please let me explain. I think you have great value in the process. I just don't like the dance of a marketing company taking over the relationship for the purpose of selling the client a bunch of collateral material, ad space, and air time. Some marketing companies are outstanding, and I love working with them. Let me give you more clarity about what I am pitching here.

Let's look at two critical elements of the "hire the marketing company to brand us" model. First, marketing and branding companies get paid via four revenue streams. The first revenue stream is selling this process and getting paid for the research. If the organization is going into something they haven't done before or want research on potential buyers, this is valuable. But to find out what employees, clients, and you think about yourself is usually a waste of time. I believe you can answer those questions or do the research yourself.

The second way they get paid is the creative design, naming, taglines, technical writing, rules around the brand, graphic work, initial materials, presentations, Web design, social media presence and management, search engine maximization, etc. Marketing companies are good here, but I have also found a less expensive and stronger answer can come from graphic design companies. I highly suggest getting help in this area.

The third revenue stream is the continued sale of these materials with updates and new creative ideas to promote your brand. This area also includes a continued Web presence. This area of support can be successful if the sales results prove themselves. Monitor it closely, and prove the results.

The fourth way they get paid is the resale of media. They get paid for placement of radio, television, magazines, newsprint, Internet, etc. Unfortunately, many firms have this as the primary goal. They want to sell you these products and services. You have to discern what they really care about.

Some of these items are needed, but many of these items are not needed, and you might be paying a premium for items that would perform better elsewhere at a much lower cost. Graphic artists are usually less expensive than marketing company graphics design departments. Website design is usually more affordable with companies that design websites full-time. Marketing companies are valuable and can be extremely helpful in branding and marketing. I am simply advising you to look at options and see where and how to use a marketing company to support you.

The second element of the marketing company model that needs to be understood is speed. Speed of change. Speed of markets. Speed of business. Brands used to be built on the past and who you were. Brands in the modern business world are built on who you need to be to meet the future needs of your clients.

I asked another prospective client to tell me what they thought the clients, prospects, employees, and management thought of their business. This was prior to one of these expensive surveys. They still went with the survey. Everything they saw in the survey was exactly what they had thought would have been said. Here is the important message: it had nothing to do with the brand they needed to develop.

Marketing companies are not all bad. Research is not all bad. The reality is that the speed in which an industry becomes commoditized is very fast in the twenty-first century. This means that a total approach must be taken toward creating a company (and individual) brand. Looking at the past, present, and future should be part of the process. If a marketing company only wants to look at the past, run away! A good brand is one that captures the strengths of the past that need to be sustained, realizes the value that you bring to clients, and identifies a brand that gives confidence in the future.

Recently, in my research on business retention, I found that companies are putting a lot less credibility and loyalty in what you have done in the past. Look at how quickly people toss a cell phone or any technology, software, a restaurant, a car, etc. This is in a world where people supposedly hate change. I believe that the availability of getting what we want is the driver of change. Why would we stay with something that is less than what we could have if it is affordable, accessible, and better?

Our brands need to be careful not to highlight what we have done and how good we have been. Buyers are purchasing based on past, present, and future thinking. Your brand needs to show credibility from the past, an immediate ability to meet a need (or needs), and the hope and promise that you will be able to meet future needs.

Branding is complex, and you know more than you think. I bet you would know the majority of the answers to the past (who you have been), present (how you want to be perceived today), and future (how you would like to be perceived to maximize your potential). Think about it, and you will probably get well down the road toward your brand. If you need to hire a good marketing/branding company to support you in this effort, I am in complete support. Just don't let them spend a ton of your money telling you what you already know.

Chapter 8

My Brand Should Align with Our Brand

Me, Inc., Fits in We, Inc.

Patrick's father, Roger Sitkins, has been one of the thought leaders in the insurance and risk management industry for over thirty years. He is the most well-known teacher, adviser, and trainer to large insurance agencies in North America. I went to one of his classes in 2003. He taught us that we were in business for ourselves as insurance agents. Being in business for yourself was expressed in the concept of "Me, Inc." He quickly expressed that Me, Inc., is always part of We, Inc., in the insurance agency world.

Technology was not anywhere near as prominent in 2003 as it is today. New technology has advanced, and Me, Inc., is now becoming a clearer part of the company brand. The brand of a company is influenced heavily by the individuals within. A quick tweet, post, or Internet comment can boost or destroy a company. When a decision maker can look on the Internet to learn about the staff members who are going to be servicing his account, individual brands start to matter. I believe every business will soon be required to proactively manage the individual brands of its employees. People are researching the individuals of a company before they do business with them.

Individual brands will come together to become the corporate brand. A corporate brand manager will need to integrate individual brand management into the overall strategy. (We will discuss how a corporate manager will execute this strategy in the next chapter.) The individual brands will be the ultimate credibility of the company and may be the primary reason someone chooses to do business with a company. The combination of the individual brands will become the We, Inc., brand.

Recently in a three-day period, I met with a representative of a very large company, and had a meeting with a very successful innovator. Both meetings began with "Larry, I have done extensive research on you. I have watched videos, read your blogs, and studied what you and your company do." Both of these individuals had researched the company after they had researched my personal information. It was exciting to hear both of them tell me they had researched the industry and determined that they had already decided they wanted to work with me and my companies to partner on new products.

Patrick's Take: On the dangerous side of this is, of course, brand damage. Larry portrayed a positive brand online due to purposeful planning and tactics; however, the outcome could have been much different. The direct impact of Larry not managing his online brand would have been the lost opportunity with this client and the revenue that resulted from it. There would have also been an indirect cost if Larry had done a poor job of managing his brand. With all of the keynote speeches and client work that Larry does, people are undoubtedly looking him up online. If outdated, irrelevant, negative information showed up in place of the positive items that he described, there is no telling how many opportunities could be lost over the length of his career.

One illustrative example of how brand damage can occur is the story of Pete Kistler. Pete was typical of most college students. He was nearing the end of his degree and was looking for an internship. The problem was that he couldn't get one. It wasn't because he was a bad student or unskilled. No, it was because he was being mistaken for a drug dealer on Google! Talk about brand damage! These potential employers were following the trend of easily screening applicants by their search results. Obviously no company wanted to take a chance on a convicted drug dealer.

Pete asked his friend Patrick Ambron to help him "bury" these negative search results. Patrick used search engine optimization (SEO) to bring more positive and relevant information to page one of Google. By doing this, they were able to hide the drug-dealing Pete Kistler and highlight the bright, aspiring entrepreneur.

They were successful in their project and knew that others probably faced similar situations. So Pete, Patrick, and their other friend Evan did what any good entrepreneurs do. They had a need and saw no viable solution, so they created it themselves. Their service, BrandYourself. com, is a great free service that allows anyone to do basic SEO to help manage their brand online.

I signed up for it myself, even though SiliconCloud does an excellent job at SEO. It is a great service and something I consider to be another weapon in my arsenal against brand damage.

Can you see the power of what I just described? We live in a world where people make decisions on doing business with you before they ever meet you. Your brand as an individual and as a company will combine to create credibility of a brand. They make final decisions prior to doing business with you. I am certain my competition would love the two opportunities that were presented to me this week. One opportunity is with one of the world's most innovative and successful entrepreneurs. He has invented a new product for an industry that I serve. He wants to partner with our company, and the financial impact could be in the billions of dollars.

Brand management of the past was all about the company. Brand management of a company in the future will be a combination of a company brand and individual brands. The complexity of managing brands will be challenging and will take a different skill set than what the current marketing and branding people have and use today.

If we leave the branding up to individuals, businesses will see frequent failures. The chance that all the individuals in a company can and will manage their brand effectively is next to zero. Employees will not know how to manage their brand. Employees will make mistakes. Combining a corporate brand and determining how the individual brands blend to create a powerful combination will take strategy and leadership. Companies will fail over single errors (bad post on social media, lack of good information on profiles, etc.) of employees' management of their brand. Being seen on a video that goes viral could be the end of a company. The individual and corporate branding of We, Inc., and Me, Inc., will be part of the strategic objectives of the company and could turn potential brand damage into brand management.

CHAPTER 9

CORPORATE BRAND MANAGER

I had the opportunity to work with a very prominent insurance agency in Atlanta recently. We went through a training class for the management and sales team on personal and corporate branding. The CEO asked a great question at the end of the session: "How do we take all these ideas on branding and implement them in our company?" He went on to express how overwhelming it all seemed to be.

It is my belief that this is a new career opportunity. We are already seeing marketing and branding companies developing these products. However, most of them are still looking for the big dollars to manage the corporate brand. The new job that will become common in a business will be the corporate brand manager. It may be a full-time job for larger companies, and it may be a part-time job for a college student or someone who works from home.

When you look at the cost of doing nothing, it quickly reveals that this is not an option. Seventy-eight percent of people are looking up the individuals in the company before meeting with them. That percentage is going to grow fast and will eventually be close to 100 percent. This means bankers, attorneys, insurance providers, potential product distributors, and others are all going to have a brand determined by every individual who works with a client. So the cost of doing nothing in this area could be devastating.

Okay, that is the defense again. What about the offense? If brands are managed effectively, it can turn into faster and more profitable financial growth. It is a must-have strategy in a business.

People can pay less than two hundred dollars a month to get a college student to manage their brand for them. One company paid a university a small donation to the marketing department to have a project team (students) develop the initial website, blogs, video blogs, and individual brand pages on all employees in the company. This was very effective and very low cost. As long as a company has a very clear plan for managing the corporate and individual brands, and good guidelines for individual brands, a lot of talented young people out there can do a great job of managing and monitoring the brand. It is still a good idea to have someone with good strategic brand management skills monitor the process and maintain regular reviews.

On the other hand, *be careful.* Someone just making posts and adding content could hurt you. Make sure you have complete clarity on what you want to accomplish, and that may require professional help. We have seen inexperienced people trying to manage individual brands, and it has resulted in big brand damage. One executive let loose his high school daughter on managing his social media and online presence. She posted so many things every day for him that he ended up getting a brand of being on social media too much. His clients thought he wasn't working and was spending all his time in a social media addiction. A good strategy and rules are a must-have in personal brand management.

The next option is to hire an outside firm to manage your corporate and personal brands. This strategy is a very touchy subject for me to address. The problem with a large number of professional marketing firms is that they can rob you blind by doing a lot of activity (posts, pictures, blogs, tweets, etc.) and getting you zero results. Companies will show you tons of activity, including site hit activity, and can generate reports that make you feel really good. However, the results you want are more sales, increased brand awareness, proactive brand management prior to a salesperson visiting a client, or other end results.

I have seen businesses write big checks to get nothing. A company called me recently to tell me about their amazing new social media strategy and their online technology presence. They had spent $160,000 on a website, full strategic social media marketing plan, blogging setup, individual brands created on the website, social media setup, and a six-month management program. It had been about three months into the program, so I went and looked around. It was pretty! Wow, they had a beautiful stagnant website. It was a $160,000 brochure and a bunch of posts (blogs, social media pushes, etc). However, in three months they had six followers—all of whom were employees of the company. I could have helped them get a better setup for $15,000 and had thousands of followers with a more focused plan.

The best advice I can give is to ask a company to show you measurable results they have brought prior clients. Don't let them sell you based on what they "could" do for you. Make sure you talk to the companies with whom they have worked and verify the quantifiable results. "We are popular and get a lot of hits" is not good enough. A lot of games can be played in this arena. Get measurements that are clearly turning into sales, profits, and desired outcomes. Also, make sure they have a plan to manage individual brands in the company, as well. It all has to fit together.

Okay, back to the intern, college student, or part-time person to help you with brand management. As long as you have a good plan and it is clear what you want to accomplish, this low-cost strategy can work well for you. Just don't allow a lot of freedom. They don't always have enough business experience to determine good judgment. Keep tight reins on them. Listen to their ideas, and encourage them to be creative. Just make sure you see it before the creativity hits the public.

I believe this game is going to get clearer very soon. So many people are starting to see such clear results from good social media and technology strategies in managing company and individual brands, so we will be getting blueprints of success that we can follow. It is my prediction that every business-to-business company will have an internal brand management job (part- or full-time) by 2015.

CHAPTER 10

YOU CAN'T FIND ME

I spoke at a large business executive conference about personal branding. During the speech I asked how often people felt they were looked up on the Internet both professionally and personally. With a request for showing hands at different frequencies, some raised their hands at one to five times per month, a few more at six to ten times per month, and most felt like they were looked up at least eleven to twenty times a month.

I also asked the participants to raise their hand if they thought it would increase over time. One hundred percent of the people in the room raised their hand, agreeing that more and more people will be researching personal and professional relationships on the Internet prior to first meetings.

When the speech ended, a gentleman who looked to be in his midfifties came directly to the stage to meet me. I had been aware of this man during the speech because he had a look of doubt and resistance regarding the message. I expected that the man was not going to praise the brilliance of my speech. I assumed he would inform me of his experience and why I was wrong. He didn't disappoint!

The gentleman was very well dressed and gave a look of confidence as he began to speak. "Mr. Linne, I would like to introduce myself" (I won't use his name). "I completely agree with the comments and points you made in your speech. However, when you were talking about how often people will look us up online, I thought of something you haven't thought about!"

His bait intrigued me. I asked him to "please, enlighten me."

He said, "I laughed when you were speaking, because I thought, 'If someone looks me up online, they won't find anything!' I guess my brand is pretty safe. I don't do any social media, online pictures or videos, no Web page, nothing." His chest was out a bit now. "So what do you think of that?"

I was in a hurry to leave the event, so I decided to respond to this gentleman in a way that would make my point quickly but leave him speechless.

"Sir, I am impressed," I began. "I have a game I like to play with individuals in my audiences. Would you mind if I played it with you?"

He showed a bit of fear in his face but responded positively. "Okay, sure."

I continued, "I would like to take a shot at defining your brand."

He stood up tall and had that smirky, salesman, know-it-all look. He said, "Take your best shot."

"Okay, here it goes. You are a salesman near the end of your career. You used to be successful but have not experienced the same level of success you enjoyed early in your career. You are not technology savvy and would not be able to react to or be proactive in working with a client if technology were required. You are seen and known as 'old school' and would struggle in selling to a modern buyer. You are a nice guy, but a large number of people probably feel sorry for you that you have stopped learning and growing." I paused. Then I asked, "How'd I do?"

He looked at me, stunned, and with a frown said, "You're probably right."

I responded, "So if others look you up on the Internet and can't find you, it helps to identify your brand."

"Touché!" he said as he simulated a knife going into his gut. "I guess you got me there. I better get busy on my brand."

He gave me a handgun shot and a wink. Again, his brand was defined even more as he walked away.

Patrick's Take: Your brand is extremely vulnerable online. It's true, if you can't be found online, then, yes, you are unfortunately promoting a negative brand. However, real brand damage can also happen when the search results of your name return very negative information as well.

Shortly after we moved into one of our office complexes, I did research on all the other companies in our building. I wanted to see who our neighbors were, and I was also curious about their digital presence. A great prospecting idea for a digital marketer, right? Most had a decent Web presence, but there was one company that stood out. When I searched the company name, I expected the usual results, like a website, some social media profiles, and other directory listings. What I found was completely different. The entire first page of Google returned results of the CEO and his sexual discretions. I was horrified. First, it immediately made me nervous to have my son around the office building. Next, I was shocked that no one in the company had done anything to proactively manage this. Most of the news stories and results were several years old. Not only did I not approach them to help, but I wondered how many potential clients have seen this information and refused to do business with them.

It doesn't really matter what is available on the Internet. What matters is knowing what is available and making the right decisions regarding the expression of your brand. Inclusion and omission are part of your brand. What you wear, what you say, what you drive, where you go, your Internet footprint (or not), and *anything* that influences how someone will think about you are your brand.

You may not want to be found on the Internet. That is okay, as long as you are okay with how that impacts your brand.

CHAPTER 11

YOUR INTERNAL BRAND

I was working with a group of salespeople recently on a project to increase their sales results. We worked through many concepts, but personal branding really hit home with one of the participants. In the middle of my teaching, he blurted out, "I know why I am struggling! I manage what people think of me outside of this office every day. I focus on getting the world of clients and prospects to think certain things about me. My problem is I do *nothing* to manage what people think of me inside the office."

He was correct. He had time management problems and external brand problems, because the people on his internal teams didn't like him and frequently spoke negatively about him in public. His assistant would roll her eyes and give negative comments about him to clients. His brand was negative because he didn't realize he had to manage his brand internally.

He has taken a 180-degree turn since this discussion. He was able to get clarity around his desired internal brand. He changed behaviors and spent more time working on the items that needed to change. He spent more time and energy with his team to help them get to know him better and understand his values and his deeper self. He also spent more time getting to know them as people (part of the brand he wanted to have). He was in such a big hurry to manage what clients and prospects thought of him, he didn't realize how important and valuable it was for internal people to know him in that same way. He knows it is going to take a long time to change this brand. He also realizes if he doesn't, he will never reach his potential.

An internal brand will determine your workload, what you receive in communication, your promote-ability, your potential trust, the response to your requests, and a lot more. What do people think of you inside of your organization? If you are a "get it done" person, more work will come your way. If you are a person who makes it hard for people to give you information, you won't get much information. I worked for a manager early in my career, and every time I gave him a report he would turn around and give me numerous projects based on that report. His brand was "when he gets information he causes more work for others." So I stopped giving him reports. He would get frustrated when he couldn't get the information, but his frustrations were easier to deal with than the huge workload he would give me when I did give him reports. This manager probably wishes he could get more information, but he won't, as long as his brand is that he will cause more work.

If you don't get things done, others may not get things done for you. If you don't get things done, you may not get high-quality projects given to you. That could impact your promote-ability. Your internal brand will determine the success of your job.

I can go through every person I have ever worked with and define his or her internal brand (at least from my perspective). I can also tell you how their brand impacted their growth and struggles while they were in the organization. Since we defined a brand as "what people think of you," we could all identify the brands of our coworkers.

The challenge is not to identify someone else's brand. The challenge is identifying our own internal brand and our desired internal brand.

Identifying our current brand requires honest feedback from others, good self-analysis, and frequent reviews. However, it is worthless if we don't completely clarify what we want people to think of us.

I found this to be so powerful for me this past year that I wrote keywords on a piece of paper and posted it on the wall in front of me in my office. These four words where what I wanted people to think of me as the leader of my companies. I believe people think these four things of me now, because I looked at them and was constantly reminded to be that person.

As you develop your brand, make sure to recognize you have an internal and external brand. Manage both, and you will increase productivity and overall success.

Internal versus External

One of my longtime clients asked me to work on some growth strategies in his business. We looked at a lot of areas and found that corporate and personal branding needed a lot of work. We spent time developing strategies and tactics to improve their brand.

When we finished, he dropped his head and said, "I don't have time to do all of this. Which of these two—corporate or personal branding—is more important? I will do that one first, and if I get the time, I will do the other one."

My response was not what he wanted to hear. I could not give a reason for either one to be more valuable or important than the other. An individual could damage his company and put him out of business in a day. His company brand was critical to delivering the right message to the market about who they were and what they did.

My advice was to find something else that was less important and make sure these two items were moved to the top of the list. He wasn't happy with his current results, so I asked him what the cost of doing nothing would be. He understood and acted.

The results have been excellent. They have increased their sales, and the individual salespeople are thriving. They have resurrected the sales of many of their staff just through creating strong personal branding.

When I started my first management job in 1988, I had a VP tell me, "You can't solve all your problems with revenue . . . but you can sure cover up a bunch of them." Corporate and personal branding is a step toward more revenue. It won't solve all the problems, but it will give you a chance to cover up a bunch!

It is a choice. We have a lot of risks we have to manage in our businesses. Branding is one of those risks. They are even selling insurance to assist with brand damage now (reputation risk management). It has become that prominent. We must choose which risks to spend our time on. I contend that branding may be one of our most critical risks we must manage.

CHAPTER 12

AVOIDING BRAND DAMAGE

When I was in high school, one of my friends had a very wise father. He used to tell us, "If you are willing to see what you are doing or saying on the front page of the newspaper the next day, you can probably proceed with what you are doing. If you wouldn't want it on the front page of the newspaper, *stop* . . . immediately."

I had that thought on my mind throughout most of school, and it became even more important to me as I became a business executive who was building a reputation in the market.

This wise statement applies today in a much more complex way. The reality of any of our behaviors being on Facebook, Pinterest, YouTube, Google, a viral e-mail, a viral text—the list goes on—is much greater than it was in the 1980s.

Avoiding brand damage requires a certain state of mind and some good processes. The successful state of mind is to keep the "on the front of the newspaper" mentality in the front of all your thoughts—and posts—at all times!

Here are some suggested processes that can help so you don't have to always remember:

1. Ask yourself before posting on social media, "How will this impact my brand?"

2. Have someone review your Internet presence on a weekly or monthly basis. My wife, my kids, my employees, Patrick, and friends all know how important brand management is to me. They all look out for me and give me quick feedback, whether it's positive or negative, about what I show on the Internet. You can also pay someone who understands brand management to observe and give you regular feedback on your online presence. If you do an online search for "online presence monitoring," you'll receive numerous pages of people and companies that provide that service.

3. Don't allow someone else to manage your brand online unless you have complete confidence in that person's understanding of your brand.

These ideas will help. However, the best way to avoid brand damage is to have a clear picture of what you want people to think of you, and maintain an attitude that everything you do will communicate a brand message to others.

Brand Damage
It's Personal!

Patrick Sitkins's Version

"In its simplest form, branding is *what people think of you*. It is
the culmination of several complex strategies, interactions, media,
communications, experiences, and relationships all boiled down into a
very clear and very real opinion of you."
—Patrick Sitkins

"You have a brand if anyone can answer the question, 'What do you
think of [insert your name]?'"
—Patrick Sitkins

CHAPTER 13

GETTING KICKED OUT
OF THE NEST

At twenty-four years old I decided to enter my next career. After a stint in financial services, and then a marketing position, I decided that it might finally be time to take a position in the family business. My dad, who was the CEO of Sitkins International at the time, had dreamed of me one day joining the company. We had discussed the possibility of my going to work with him on several occasions, but the timing was never right for me. Larry had joined the company a year prior to this, and it looked like things were really picking up. I saw some of the exciting directions the company had taken and decided it was time to consider joining the team.

I vividly remember calling my dad at his office. I was in the parking lot of the oral surgeon's office while Dianne (my girlfriend at the time) was getting her wisdom teeth pulled. It seemed appropriate to call the office line, which was not the norm. This was, after all, a very important call. I got through reception and began telling him that I had been doing a lot of thinking, and I thought it was time that we opened up discussions again. He was pleasantly surprised. We set plans for me to have several conversations with him and Larry separately. After that, it was decided. I was the newest addition to the Sitkins team, and I had no idea what that really meant. One of the important items that we implemented right away was the separation of business and family issues. In alignment with that, Larry would be my mentor, and I was his direct report and responsibility. Roger/Dad was not my boss.

This is going to be great, I thought to myself. *My dad is extremely excited, and Larry seems more than willing to mentor me. If those two guys are behind me, this is going to be easy.*

We decided that it would make sense for me to get firsthand experience of what the company did. Before I had even packed up my things to move to Fort Myers, Florida, they sent me to a high-end producer program that they were hosting in Tampa. I left Jacksonville Beach, optimistic, excited, and anxious. When I checked in at the hotel, there was an envelope waiting for me. It was from Larry. *Cool! He's probably written to let me know how great it is that I'm here and how excited he is to work with me.* I made my way up to my room, set down my things, and opened the letter that was written on the Renaissance Hotel letterhead.

Patrick,

I am glad you are here and on the team. Today will begin an awesome journey! Please read the attached. I will meet you @ 6:30 am for breakfast prior to the session.

See you there!

Larry

This was a good start. Larry threw in a few encouraging words and exclamations. *Nice. Did that say 6:30 a.m.? Is he insane?* The only time I got up that early was for a dawn-patrol surf session or fishing, not for a breakfast meeting.

I flipped the page and read the attachment. The rest of his message to me was a little different from what I expected. Without going into too much detail, here are the bullet points of his message:

- Humility is a key with employees and members (clients).
- Take notes and ask questions later.
- Dad is called Roger!
- Members will only see potential if they see appropriate confidence and determination.
- Ask good questions.
- You must learn to do and learn to teach.
- It is okay to say "I don't know," but do it with confidence.
- You are at a distinct disadvantage because of your last name. We will have to work hard to overcome that.

Wait a minute, a "distinct disadvantage"? Humility? Dad is no longer "Dad"? What's going on here? Not only was I going to have to work harder than anyone in our company to gain the trust of our employees and clients, but, as I would soon learn, nobody really expected me to succeed. It was clear that managing people's perceptions not only was the foundation to my success but also the only thing that mattered early on.

We had a great breakfast meeting at 6:30 a.m. the next morning. After two days of sitting in and observing the session, I had learned a lot from my first event with Sitkins International. I was even more excited and more anxious than I was before. A few weeks later, I packed my things and moved down to Fort Myers.

For the next two years, Larry and I met weekly to discuss the business and our client's business, we worked on business acumen, but most importantly we worked on my brand.

Every time I showed visible progress, like advancing my teaching, facilitating, or speaking skills, or when I brought more value, Roger would always say, "Looks like we are finally kicking you out of the nest." It was a big joke among Roger, Larry, and me (truthfully more for Roger than any of us). Looking back on it, every time I got "kicked out" brought me closer to my desired brand. I guess it was a good thing after all.

During my six years at Sitkins International, I had the unique opportunity to work with Larry on our company rebranding, help many of our clients brand or rebrand themselves, build our employee personal brands, and most directly help each other build and implement our own personal branding strategies. During my time at Sitkins International, I had to work extremely hard to build a powerful yet different personal brand. I could not be the same as Roger or Larry. I had to be genuine in who I was and the value I brought, but it had to be different. As my experience and expertise deepened, I began to focus more and more on my passions. This eventually led to my becoming one of the leading marketing and branding consultants in the insurance industry.

Now I continue daily to build upon the brand that I started to build at the age of twenty-four (I am now in my thirties). There is no doubt in my mind that I could not have had near the success that I did at Sitkins International—and now with my company SiliconCloud—without a very purposeful personal branding approach.

I was thrilled that Larry, my mentor and someone for whom I have great respect, asked me to coauthor this book with him. I have seen the results that these strategies have had for me, for him, for our employees, for our clients, and hopefully now for you!

CHAPTER 14

WHAT PEOPLE THINK OF YOU

As mentioned in the introduction, we have helped brand hundreds of companies and individuals over the years. We have executed extremely creative and complex strategies that we turn into very simple tactical execution. Through all of this, we have learned a lot about what works and what does not. We have seen the trends, and we are convinced that personal branding is critical in modern business practices. We realize the urgency that people are starting to feel, and we also see the "chicken with its head cut off" reaction that typically happens when they try to develop a brand and manage it.

So what is a brand? There are many (too many) definitions of branding. It is a topic that has been written about, researched, guessed at, and consulted on for years. According to Wikipedia, the term "personal branding" was first introduced in *Think and Grow Rich* in 1937. The idea resurfaced in the early eighties in the book *Positioning: The Battle for Your Mind*, and then became widely popular because of a Tom Peters article in 1997. Since then, a plethora of information and resources have been created, making branding extremely complex and hard to understand. There are dozens of definitions, hundreds of branding companies, even more self-proclaimed experts and gurus, and countless resources on the subject. When we first started writing this book over a year ago, the term "branding" would return 119,000,000 results on Google, and Yahoo! and Bing each returned 25,900,000 results. Now, "branding" has 150,000,000 results from Google, Yahoo! with 133,000,000, and Bing with 126,000,000 results. It's no wonder that individuals and companies typically misunderstand and avoid this topic. Taking all of these resources and trying to filter them down to a simple explanation can be overwhelming. Even if you have a good feel for the subject, translating that into personal branding, determining your brand items, differentiating yourself, and managing that brand effectively can be a daunting task.

Branding is usually seen as a "nice to have" item, not a must-have. Because of this, it really becomes a B priority at best. Usually it is something that is thought about, but very rarely are concrete plans put in place. People tend to have a good brand and may know what they should be doing, but it is usually the act of organizing their thoughts and action items that never gets done. There seems to be too much to do and not enough time. Most just throw their hands in the air and say, "I quit." As shown above, it is not the lack of information on this subject that prevents people from managing a powerful brand—there is certainly enough of that. It's navigating all of the chaos and confusion to bring calm, clarity, and control to the process.

So let's bring some clarity to this extremely complex subject. As stated in the preface, branding, as we define it, is *what people think of you*. In its simplest form, that's what it is. It is the culmination of several complex strategies, interactions, media, communications, experiences, and relationships all boiled down into a very clear and very real opinion of you.

Some people worry about this. They may not like what their current brand is and think that there is nothing they can do about it. The intriguing thing about a brand is that it is just as realistic to improve a brand as it is to damage one. What you have read so far, the following chapters, and our examples provide evidence of this.

CHAPTER 15

"I DON'T HAVE A BRAND"

We hear it a lot. People swear to us that they don't have a brand, and they believe it because they have never thought about their brand. Oftentimes they say something along the lines of "I'm just me. I don't have a brand, and I don't need one." That is truly incorrect thinking. You have a brand if anyone can answer the question, "What do you think of [insert your name]?"

My wife, Dianne, has a great brand, and that was one of the initial things I noticed about her. She is extremely intelligent, driven, competitive, caring, compassionate, and family-oriented. People love being around her because she is fun and also an amazing friend. She is always willing to help others and puts people before herself. I honestly don't know anyone who doesn't like her. She is a tremendous athlete and a leader.

I would be willing to put a large amount of money down that says if we asked her coworkers, friends, or family what they think of her, they would give almost an identical response. The reason I believe that is simple. Her brand is clear to those around her. She knows exactly who she is and who she is not. She is strong in her convictions, and she makes decisions based on what she believes in. This is communicated in her actions and interactions. Her brand items are also powerful and positive. But she will swear to you that she doesn't have a personal brand.

As Larry and I began writing this book, I told her about the concept and importance of the topic. She said, "That is so 'businessy.' Your clients will love it." She is a marine scientist by education and an officer in the US Coast Guard Reserves. Business to her is guys in suits, meeting all day. Boring. She would much rather be on a boat, busting bad guys, cleaning up oil spills, or doing anything other than sitting in meetings. Branding to her is as focused on business as balance sheets and conferences. In her mind, it is best left to the guys in suits to focus on.

I explained to her that our intended audience is anyone, not just someone "in business." As we discussed it further, I tried to take branding out of the business box and open it up in a broader context. We talked about what people think of you and reputation. Those concepts were much clearer and drove the idea home. We discussed what she believes in, who she is, what she likes, and what people would say if asked about her. It became clear that she not only had a brand, but it was also being communicated very clearly. Even though she didn't see it as managing her brand, she is still very proactive in managing people's perceptions about her.

The point here is this: No matter how hard you focus on or ignore branding, you have one. You may believe that ignorance is bliss, and if you don't think about it then you won't have to deal with it. Just because you may choose to ignore your brand and live in a state of denial doesn't mean that your brand isn't being communicated every day. Just as it is easy for me and others to communicate Dianne's personal brand, people can communicate your brand, as well.

Everyone has a brand. That's a fact. Whether you like it or not, you have been managing a set of perceptions and telling people all of your life exactly what you want them to think about you.

People use excuses and try to ignore their brand because of the complexities listed above. It's too overwhelming, so instead of dealing with it, they try to hide from it. They think by ignoring it, it will just go away. Whether you are a CEO, a college student, a salesperson, a burger flipper, military personnel, a professional athlete, or a politician, the fact remains the same. You have a brand. There is a choice, of course. You can either proactively manage your brand or allow others to tell you what it is.

CHAPTER 16

IT'S A BEAST!

First, I need to acknowledge that life is overwhelming, whether it is business, personal, or otherwise. We are not suggesting that personal branding is something new in that regard. What we are stating though is the fact that it is overwhelming. We know from firsthand experience that this whole concept can be friend and foe all at the same time.

We got firsthand experience of the overwhelming nature of all this on a personal branding project, specifically focusing on media management, with one of our clients. They are an extremely successful independent insurance brokerage firm in Eastern Canada. They are well-known, well respected, intelligent, and innovative. The purpose of our session was to focus on their branding strategy for both their specialties and employees. They have some very specific niches, such as ski resorts, summer resorts, rafting programs, and golf and country clubs, and they are seen as experts in those areas. The CEO's desire was to expand their presence in those spaces and to promote the individual expertise of their employees in those areas.

We have worked with this brokerage firm for several years now. They have sat through countless online sessions, calls, and live presentations about branding and brand management. They have heard us discuss branding and the importance of it in an organization and individuals. We didn't have to work on selling the importance of this to her. She and the organization understood the concept and had bought in. As we discussed their current situation and desired end in mind, we could tell that the CEO was struggling a bit. She was very agreeable with what we were discussing, yet she seemed a bit frustrated.

At one point she stopped me and said, "I completely buy-in to all of this, and I know branding and media management is crucial to our success in these niches, but it's a beast. Seriously, it's just a beast." It was pretty clear that she was overwhelmed. She was a victim of what we discussed earlier. The massive amount of information (some coming from our messages over the years) and items to implement became an overwhelming and complex list of things to do.

As with any large project, we like to use the old analogy of eating an elephant. The only way to eat an elephant is one bite at a time. That is what we had to do. We began looking at the current brand of the brokerage firm and the employees in the marketplace. Then we determined the best-case scenario and their future brand items. After establishing that clarity, we built out specific action items. They now had a plan with prioritized action items and a clear vision of how to implement—one bite at a time.

This story makes branding seem doable, and it can be—with a plan. However, this "beast," as our client put it, is big. And worse, it has teeth. The whole idea of branding can include easily managed items, short-term fixes, long-term strategies, future strategies, tactics that take time and resources, media, social media and the complexity that brings, images, videos, thirty-second commercials or elevator speeches, the way you dress, items that support the brand, items that destroy it, trying to align with your organization's brand, and managing it with clients, employees, key contacts, etc. *Breathe.*

The trick to taming this beast is to determine your powerful brand items, manage what people think of you proactively (we will discuss how), and do this by focusing on the key items to communicate your brand.

CHAPTER 17
THE PLAN

Why?

Most people who have spent time around young children know the "why" stage. This typically happens right around three years old. During this highly frustrating time (for parents), children begin to question everything. They not only question the ways of the world but also every statement that they hear. The questioning isn't designed to intentionally annoy everyone around them; it's more a genuine interest in why things are the way they are. They also want to know why they have to do what they are told. Luckily for parents, they grow out of this phase; however, this is also an unfortunate occurrence. As we grow older, we lose some of that curiosity that we once had. We begin to conform and stop challenging with "Why?"

As you develop your plan, continue to ask yourself, "Why?" Challenge your brand, challenge your brand items, and challenge your plan.

What Is a Plan?

Simply put, a plan is a map to help you get to where you want to go. The planning process looks at your current situation, its potential, and its future, and then lays out specifics steps to get you there.

A personal branding plan should have those elements in it. First, you need to assess your current situation. You should look at your current reputation in the marketplace to get a good idea of what message you have been sending. Next, you need to go through the exercise of determining your future brand. Finally, develop action items to get you there. Let's look at each of these in more detail.

Assessment

As stated above, this is the first step in developing a plan. This process is typically the toughest step. It is usually very difficult to be honest with ourselves. Starting with the assessment, we believe there are three categories that should be looked at to determine your current situation: brand management, media utilization, and social media. Let's look at each of these.

Brand Management

This category encompasses the bigger picture. Some questions to consider in this category are:

- Do you have a core list of brand items identified?
- Are you a connector? What is your specialty? At what do you excel? What value do you bring to relationships?
- Are those items differentiated, or are they similar to everyone else?

Being friendly, hardworking, and tech savvy are not different. Most people could say the same things about themselves. The idea here is to set yourself apart from the rest of the pack.

- Are your peers in alignment with your desired brand?

As you will see a little later in Chapter 18, who you associate with both online and offline can greatly impact your brand.

- Are you in alignment with your organization?
- Your school, team, or company has a set of values and a brand. Are you in alignment with those? You need to believe in those values and agree with that brand.
  Is your organization in alignment with you?

This is crucial, especially if you are in a leadership position inside of that organization. Your job should be to create a personal brand so powerful and positive that the organization is drawn toward it. Try to push your organization to more clearly define their brand, and you should be seen as an integral part of the organization's brand.

- Do you have multiple ways to communicate your brand?
- Do you utilize items, like social and other media, to communicate your brand?

To effectively manage your brand, you need to be purposeful in everything you do, ensuring that you are communicating the same brand message, whether is if online or offline. This category is really the foundation for everything else. Without a clear set of brand items, it is almost impossible to proactively manage an effective brand.

Media Utilization

Media can be any communication portal. This can refer to the Internet, traditional media outlets, websites, images, video, etc. Media should be seen as one way to manage your personal brand, not the only way. In the first category, brand management, there are certainly items that do not fall under media. Of course, this is still a very important piece. Some questions to consider here are:

- Are you easy to find?

This is especially important if you have a common name or company name. For example, if your name is Joe Smith or Jane Doe, it will be much harder for someone to find the Joe that they are looking for. As with the BrandYourself.com example, it could be very damaging if someone is looking for you but finds the wrong Joe.

- Do you have a good defense in place to monitor your brand? (We will cover this in detail in the next section.)
- Do you have consistency in the message across all media?

Your brand message needs to be the same across all media. Look to incorporate a standard tagline or bio, profile picture, brand items, etc.

- Is media enhancing your brand, or is it damaging?
- Do pictures, videos, and other media portray the brand that you are trying to convey? For example, if you are looking to be viewed as a leader with strong morals, it would probably be very damaging to have pictures surface of you at a gentleman's club.

The final category is the newer piece of the puzzle.

Social Media

We are all social by nature. The genius of what social media platforms do is that it allows us to relate, connect, and network the way we always have; these applications just make it easier. Social media include blogging and conversations, the well-known Facebook, Twitter, and LinkedIn, as well as other social platforms like Google+, Pinterest, etc. Some items to consider with social media are:

- Are you utilizing these platforms to enhance your brand message?
- Is there consistency in the powerful message across all social media?
- Are you a proactive communicator or passive listener?
- Are your profiles up-to-date, error-free, and clearly communicated? It should be easy to see where you go to school or work, and your experience should be up-to-date. It should be easy to identify what you do, what you like, and what you stand for. Your profiles should also be free of grammar and spelling errors. Just because it's online doesn't mean that it is okay to be sloppy with language.

Future Brand Management

Once you have a good handle on your current situation and understand why you need to enhance your brand, the next step is to determine the potential. What do you want others to think about you? What powerful statements and thoughts do you want someone to associate with you? How will this help you? What would that mean?

There are several ways to go about this. Look at industry leaders, successful people, mentors, or those whom you look up to. What items do you see? Can you emulate some of them? Look to those who are ahead of you in your organization, at school, etc. What items do you see? What items do others see?

Determine your goals in life: career, family, legacy, etc. What brand items will help you get there faster and ensure that you reach them?

Brand Planning: From Who? to How?

Once you have done an assessment of your current brand, the next step is to begin building out your plan. Below is a simple blueprint to ensure that you have a proactive approach without wasting your time simply doing activities.

Who?

The key starting point for any strategy is to ask the following questions: To whom are you trying to appeal? Are you looking to connect with clients or prospects, or both? Are you looking for a job, seeking out employees, or looking for a date? Who is your demographic? Digital presence and social media allow you to target specific groups in a way that was never possible offline. The best strategies are built on specific target markets, so you need to decide whom to target before you figure out how to do it.

You also need to decide who will be on your team. Let's face it, your plan will fail if you try to do it all on your own. The functions to consider in building your personal branding team are:

- Leadership (this better be you). You must be the ultimate decision maker on your personal brand. Yes, you can build a team and have others manage some of the functions necessary, but you still have to control the process.
- Strategy (if you don't know how to get to your future brand, then this will be critical to find). This is in the plan. What are the

steps to enhance your current brand, build your future brand, and break any negative brand items that exist?

- Content. Blogging and content creation are keys to any marketing program today. The same goes with a personal branding strategy. Your content can be original posts or comments, reposting, or discussing current world or industry events. It could also be videos, songs, etc. If you aren't wired to sit down and write content, then you should consider either hiring someone to help you or finding creative ways to engage in conversations online.

- Creativity/graphics. This is a higher-end item but something to consider. Especially in the social media world, having an aesthetically pleasing profile and website/blog is important. Having a personal logo or brand identity and a professional-looking website/blog, and creating infographics and other items may be a bit too much if you are just starting your personal branding approach, but they are things to consider.

- Technology. Just as we described in Chapter 16, this can all be overwhelming. Technology can certainly enhance your brand, but it brings a lot of complexity to this, as well. Having someone on your team who understands current and emerging technology will greatly help. He or she should be able to help you decide what to use and what not to use, and help you determine your best ROI on technology.

What?

One of the biggest issues here is that most people haven't identified what success looks like—in other words, documenting what has to happen in order for you to be happy with your progress.

Where?

Where will you invest your time, energy, and resources to get the maximum return? Also, where will you participate? There are hundreds of places where you can have a presence. The trick is to determine the ideal locations that will have the greatest impact for you. Your best bet on "where" is going to be determined by what you are trying to accomplish. If you are trying to manage your brand with your family, friends, and close acquaintances, then Facebook and Google+ could be good places to participate. If you are looking to manage your brand with employees, employers, or any other business contacts, then you would probably want to consider LinkedIn or a personal blog.

There really is no magic pill or right answer here. Just look to see where your target audience participates the most, and go to that platform.

When?

Develop a proactive and systematic schedule. Consistency here is the key. There are a bunch of very good studies that focus on when the best time of day and best days are to post items. The most diligent research and most compelling data come from my friends at HubSpot. They have published numerous studies, white papers, and stats that guide any person or company on what, when, and how to post. They have over seven thousand companies with which they work, and the data that comes from this sample is extremely valuable.

One of the most simplistic yet beneficial segments in most of their research is the differentiation between personal and corporate, and business-to-business and business-to-consumer markets. If you go to www.hubspot.com, you can view a lot of their awesome stats, reports, and resources.

Every sector and region is slightly different, so test your market to find the right mix.

Why?

We covered this above, but to expand, this should be asked before you do anything online, corporately or personally. "Why am I posting or sending this?" You should be able to answer this question with an honest appraisal of its value. "Because I like it" is not enough in business; you need to have a genuine motive. If it doesn't provide value or get people thinking or talking, then why post it?

How?

Once you have thought through the questions above, you should be ready to develop a plan, no matter how simple or complex, for your digital marketing strategy.

Execution

Once you have your current and future brand clear in your mind, next you have to develop build and break plans. What are the items that you need to build your brand up, and what are the things that you need to stop?

- What will enhance you brand or move you to your future brand?
- What items will damage or deter your success?
- What are some "have to" tactics that are nonnegotiable?

In this last part, it is crucial to be as detailed as possible. It also helps to document this process. If you are looking for a practical guide and example of how to build a personal branding plan, as well as other resources, visit www.siliconcloud.com/branddamage.

CHAPTER 18

DEFENSE

A Defense Can Lose the Game

Larry talked about offense. He was the offense guy in football. I was the pitcher when I played baseball at Jacksonville University. My job was to keep people from scoring. So Larry asked me to address defense.

The excitement from sporting events comes from action: the walk-off home runs, eighty-yard touchdown runs, buzzer-beating three-pointers, and penalty kicks. Most spectators don't go to watch a shutout from the home team pitcher, a great performance from the defensive line, or a brilliantly executed flat back four in soccer. The glory is almost always in the offense. Most sports have proven in the past few years that offense will clearly win games. However, defenses have proven they can lose games, as well. The same goes for personal branding.

Protecting your brand through defensive strategies may be just as important as having good offensive strategies. You can have a fantastic set of differentiating brand items, a top-notch communication strategy, and the most positive reputation around. Without a defensive process to complement this, your offense could fizzle. One negative interaction, one instant, or one misstep can damage everything.

Jenga

Imagine a Jenga game with all the blocks stacked high. If you have ever played this game, then you know how fragile this stack of blocks can be. Every block is stacked carefully, crisscrossed and all interdependent. In case you haven't played, the objective is to take turns removing one block at a time. You can remove any block you like, from any level. As the game goes on, the stack becomes more and more unstable. Most times it takes several moves or removals of blocks to finally get the stack to crumble. However, at any point, one mistake, one error, or one miscalculation can send the entire stack crashing down. If your move knocks over the stack, then you lose.

Now imagine that this represents your branding strategy. Every individual block represents a different strategy or tactic. They represent the hours spent on determining your future brand, the media in place to support it, your Internet footprint that you've worked so hard to manage, and your reputation in your marketplace or circle of influence. As with the real game, one false move could cause you to lose, causing your whole strategy to crumble.

What's worse, other people are trying to sabotage your game, as well. So not only do you need to be extremely careful in managing your own strategy, you also need to constantly be aware of what others are doing. If you aren't monitoring your game (branding strategy), someone else could come in and ruin the game for you. They could post damaging content about you, they could trash you in a blog post or Tweet, or they could take a statement you make the wrong way. Without you realizing it, the market may be getting a very incorrect message about you, damaging your reputation. Some basic strategies can include having a third party review all your media prior to placing it in public, getting a proofreader, outsourcing your writing, having a PR or digital marketing company on retainer in case of a major negative event, frequently doing searches on yourself to see what others are saying/posting about you, and ultimately asking yourself that important question before doing or communicating anything in public media: "How will this impact what others think of me?" We will address a more specific defensive strategy later in this chapter.

Lesson from a Casino Mogul

Years ago, casino mogul Stephen Wynn made an interesting comment during a keynote speech at a Charles Schwab conference. He said that it only takes one poor client experience to ruin an entire company. This seems like a huge claim coming from a man who owns several of the top casinos on the Vegas Strip. He has thousands of customers pour through his doors every day. How could he possibly think that one, just one, poor experience could ruin his entire organization? Simple. It's the same principle as Jenga. One damaging experience at the wrong time and wrong place could have a rippling (and crippling) effect on your brand, leaving it irreparable.

Birds of a Feather

I referred to this earlier. Often overlooked in branding are the people, groups, organizations, and events to which you are connected. Who and what you choose to connect with says a lot about who you are. These connections can either enhance people's perception of you, or they can severely damage your brand. As they say, birds of a feather flock together.

One of my friends told me an amazing story about the power of connections. His former roommate from school connected with him on Facebook. He hadn't talked to the guy since they were in school together but thought it would be good to see what he was up to. Very shortly after connecting with him, his old roommate went through his entire friend list and connected with all of the attractive women on his list, including his fiancée. These women saw the requests and thought it was one of my buddy's good friends, so most accepted the request.

It became very clear that this guy had a lifestyle that didn't match up with my friend's brand. He was connecting with bondage and porn sites, and he was responding to events such as an S-M conference in Vegas. My friend was horrified to see these online behaviors. The fact that many of his female friends saw these behaviors, as well, became quite a challenge for him. They began to ask him about this guy and wondered why they were friends. My buddy had to play defense and explain that they were roommates in school and not true friends. This activity made people question my friend (though it didn't have any lasting effects, as he is very good at managing his own brand), so he deleted his old roommate as an online friend. He didn't want to be associated with this kind of behavior or lifestyle. Even though it wasn't my friend who was doing these things, it still trickled to him based on his connection with his old roommate.

Your connections can either enhance what you are trying to portray, or they can hurt you.

Defensive Game Plan

So what are some ways to play defense?

Do an Analysis

As mentioned earlier, words, actions, thoughts, appearance, interactions, etc., either support or damage your brand. A good exercise is to determine what items support or enhance your brand and what items damage your brand. To do this, simply split a sheet of paper into two columns. Label the columns "What enhances my brand" and "What damages my brand." Think about voice tonality, posture, posts you make, information you share with others, your peer group, how you behave at work, and what is communicated about you outside of work. Place those current items in the appropriate columns.

Next, develop build and break plans. What should you do on a regular basis to maintain your brand? What more could you be doing? And what should you avoid or stop? Create a list of action items.

Regular Audits

Just like the Jenga game, you have to be in control of your moves. You cannot allow others to ruin your strategy for you. You have to be the one in control. Items to constantly be aware of are what is being said and what information can be linked to you. If you are aware of what the marketplace is receiving about you, then you can react quickly and make adjustments or support the information.

Technology can certainly help you here. Try setting up alerts on your name, company, competitors, and organizations that you are involved with. See what is being said about you, both good and bad. If you are playing good defense, then you will always be several steps ahead. Careful monitoring of items such as pictures, videos, articles, and comments is crucial.

Another real risk is someone hacking your accounts and spamming your contacts or sending viruses or damaging content. You need to minimize your risk of being hacked. You certainly don't want someone going out there and representing you negatively. Remember, information moves fast.

Outsource

It is becoming very affordable to have someone manage and monitor your brand. The return on investment can be well worth it. Having someone spend time on your brand weekly to check the market and monitor your brand could pay for itself by avoiding one negative event.

If you aren't monitoring your brand and media, it could have a lasting damaging impact.

Chapter 19

Brand Examples

Anti-Holism

One of Aristotle's many famous quotes is "The whole is greater than the sum of its parts." This idea has been adapted to describe everything from landscape design to team dynamics and nearly everything in between. In researching this topic, I even found two additional theories that describe this: holism and reductionism. One resource stated that holism is simply the definition of what Aristotle thought. It also said that no one in his right mind could reject holism.

We have gone mad.

In a moment of unintentional insanity, we have come up with anti-holism. We are suggesting that personal branding's importance today is a situation where the parts are indeed greater than the whole. Aristotle would not be happy with us. The market's acceptance and trust of the parts over the whole is not new. As Larry has already demonstrated, and as you will see in this section, this has been done with music groups, endorsements, and even big corporations. The parts, in many instances, have been bigger than the whole. With a clear understanding of how the market reacts to the individuals in an organization, we can now harness the power of proactive brand management.

Below are some examples of strong personal brands. We have listed several *whole* and *parts*. Some of them are very well-known, and some are not. What we hope to illustrate is that some individuals stand out more than others, and trust in the *whole* was generated almost entirely by one *part*. The parts are what ultimately led to the whole's success.

We will start with some easy ones to get your mind in the right place.

Chrysler

Try to name one other person on the executive team during the Lee Iacocca era.

Brazil

Name one other national soccer team player besides Pelé between 1958 and 1970.

'N Sync

Justin Timberlake was the most well-known member of this five-person boy band. His brand elevated their success, and he later separated himself from the group to start a solo career. The group never made another album, and JT was the only one to have high-level continued success.

Strategic Coach

Strategic Coach is a business/entrepreneur coaching organization located in Canada. They are an intellectual capital machine that creates more useful tools than you could ever use in your lifetime. Dan Sullivan is the founder of the organization, and he is the brand. Early on, people would go to Strategic Coach classes to learn from Dan. As the programs became more popular, he hit a plateau. The demand for classes quickly became greater than his time would allow. He has done a great job of bringing other highly talented facilitators in, but he is still the brand. In order to get Dan, you have to pay a premium. He as the *part* is still greater than the *whole* that is the organization.

Even though he is still the premium brand, the individual facilitators have done a great job of developing their brand in the marketplace. Now participants not only choose to attend a Strategic Coach class because of the facilitators, but they also choose to attend or not attend a class based on the facilitators. They have a sense of who the individuals are and what value they will receive by attending certain groups. The parts of Strategic Coach have brands that have allowed Dan Sullivan to maximize his brand, but now the individual brands create a bigger company brand.

Energy Drinks

The whole is not unlike every other drink. Companies like Monster Energy and Red Bull use packaging and product placement to appeal to their target audience, but what they have done better than most is their endorsement strategy. They understand that the market trusts the public figures that they idolize, so these energy giants make sure that these high-profile people choose them over their competitors. For example, Monster has looked at their target demographic and connected with athletes that appeal to them. They sponsor athletes in two-wheel dirt, two-wheel asphalt, action, snow, and water sports, and more. There were honestly too many athletes to count on their site. They also sponsor musicians, celebrities, and even the Monster girls. This strategy of promoting the parts has certainly led to the great success of the whole.

Then there's Red Bull. Their Stratos project recently was an endorsement for Felix Baumgartner to do a skydive—from space! Is Red Bull in trying to colonize Mars? Are they interested in space exploration? No. Their product is an energy drink. So why would they invest so much in a guy jumping out of a balloon? (The total amount was undisclosed, but it is clear that they put up a sizable investment.) Simple: their brand! They sell more than energy drinks; they sell an image and a lifestyle. Not only did Felix's stunt enhance this lifestyle, but Red Bull wanted to attach to his daredevil brand as well.

These Are the Things that Don't Belong

A symbol, Slim Shady, *Born Villain*, a few knights, disco stick, Young Money . . .

Not all brand items have to conform or even be fully understood. They do, however, have to be powerful. Prince, Eminem, Marilyn Manson, Kiss, Lady Gaga, and Nicki Minaj are prime examples of this. These entertainers found a way to break out of the traditional mold and brand themselves as something very unusual. They strive to do things that are considered different and strange, and they always make people question them. Whether you enjoy their music or not, one thing can't be disputed—they have found ways to completely differentiate themselves in a very crowded market. Their antics, dress, words, and presence have defied what is normal. Much of their success has undoubtedly come from their branding efforts.

Other examples of powerful personal brands in the entertainment world are Jimmy Buffett and Kenney Chesney. Both of these legends were at one point in their careers country singers. They both had mild success as traditional country acts. Their mega success didn't come until they found a creative brand that spoke to a very niche group. First Buffett and then Chesney carved out their sound, stage, and persona around the island life. They sing about boats, beaches, and bars, and they have ballads about the good life on the sand. They have created a cult following by managing a reputation that their target audience loves.

Pursue Your Passions

Mark Rollins is an insurance agent by profession, but he will tell you that he is much more than that. There is a group of very innovative agents out there, but they are unfortunately lumped in with the rest. When someone says "insurance," the response is usually immediate, powerful, and *negative*. It is extremely hard for insurance agents to brand themselves as progressive and different. For a long time, Mark was in that group of innovative agents who had a hard time convincing the marketplace that he was truly different from his competition. After years of trying, our longtime friend and client finally found the winning combination. He went with his passion and focused on his brand.

Mark is driven by helping those in need. He was actually the one who got me and countless others involved with Bridges to Community. He donates a lot of time and resources to local and global charities. He does this because he truly cares. It isn't self-serving. He finally found a way to combine his career with his passion, and NonProfit Guard was created.

Mark created a personal brand and program that focuses on helping nonprofit organizations. By differentiating himself through creative naming, packaging, content creation, and proactive management of his brand, he is now known as the nonprofit expert. He has created processes, blogs, video resources, social media, connectivity portals, and tools specifically for this niche. He is the go-to guy for risk management advice in the nonprofit world.

Fighting Dolphins

During my freshman year at Jacksonville University, our season schedule was packed full of elite top-tier baseball programs. During one of our many encounters with Florida State University, I learned an important lesson in the power of branding and reputation.

We traveled to Tallahassee to take on the Seminoles around midseason. Both teams were ranked in the Top 25 in the NCAA at the time. We were having a great year, and the Seminoles were too (they are consistently ranked in the Top 25). To accurately tell this story, I have to disclose that FSU beat us a majority of the games during my time at JU.

I was hanging out in the outfield of Mike Martin Field with several other pitchers and position players during pre-game batting practice. We were shagging balls, joking around to keep things light, and also talking about the game. One of our catchers said something that stuck with me. He said, "I was talking to some of their guys over the summer, and we were talking about both programs. They told me that there is not a huge difference between the talent in most of the Division I schools. Most programs have great players, but the difference is in attitude and prestige. There is a certain arrogance that comes with playing for a top-tier program. They know there is an intimidation factor at play every time they step on the field."

They were right. It was intimidating playing against schools that you grew up watching. They were also right about talent. Professional athletes come from a wide variety of schools, and plenty of them didn't even play

Division I. There is certainly a little well-earned respect that those top-tier players got and continue to get even after their playing days.

Talk about the power of reputation.

Motor City Bad Boy

Dennis Rodman was part of the 1989-1990 championship Detroit Pistons teams. Back then he was an extremely talented basketball player who didn't cause a lot of commotion. As his career developed, so did his brand. He went from another talented guy who blended into the rock star that he is still known as today. He began dying his hair crazy colors, wearing makeup, and dressing like a woman at times. He had an outrageous off-court reputation.

Similar to Brian Bosworth, Terrell Owens, and Ochocinco (Bengals, Patriots, and Dolphins), Dennis Rodman had a pretty negative reputation. He and the others were not people you would want your kids to emulate or aspire to be. However, they all have done something powerful; they created a clear, differentiated brand. While I don't condone much of what these guys are known for, you have to give them credit. They have found ways to create a lasting impression on the marketplace. There is some merit in that.

The Bank

I recently walked into my bank on a Friday afternoon around 2:00 p.m. Two personal bankers were up front, a manager was roaming around the lobby, and three people stood behind the desk. One of the personal bankers flagged me over as soon as I walked in the door. I sat down and told her that I would like to close one of my accounts. She simply took my card and driver's license and began to process it. There was no discussion about why I wanted to close it or if there was anything she could do to help.

As we sat silent for a few minutes, I tried to strike up a conversation. "So how are you today?"

"Well, it's Friday, so that's good," she replied without even looking away from her screen. After she finished processing my request, she stood up and told me to follow her to the counter to finalize everything. She walked me 85 percent of the way there and then turned around without saying a word. I wondered if I had done something to insult her, or maybe she was just having one of those days.

Next, I was greeted with a half smile and a monotone voice. "How can I help you?" I told her that I was closing my account and wanted to move some funds around. She got out a slip and began filling it out. While I was waiting, a man went to the window next to me. He seemed to be a regular, since he knew that girl helping me and the man next to her. First, the man asked the girl assisting me how she was. She said, "Oh, I'm okay, I guess. I'd be a lot better if I wasn't working."

Next, the man asked the other bank employee how he was. The employee responded, "It's Friday. I'll be a lot better in four hours."

I couldn't believe what I was hearing. How could this very well-known bank not have employees who were trained on attitude, communication, and client experience?

After everything was finalized, I walked toward the front door to leave. As I made my way out, I took one last glance around the lobby. Every employee, including the manager, had their heads hanging, they had slouching postures and almost-expressionless faces, and it was extremely quite.

This experience was a direct reflection on the bank's brand to me. It seemed almost exactly in alignment with the negative outlook typically placed on corporate America. Everyone was conforming, robotic in their responses, no passion for their jobs, and certainly no support from the corporate headquarters. It made me feel sorry for the employees, and it made me sad for the bank. My interaction with the employees and the bank's reputation both had a damaging effect on the bank's brand that day. Brand damage from the individuals was my experience that day. I wonder if a portion of their enormous advertising budget ($1.9 billion in 2011) would have been better allocated toward personal brand training. Based on this interaction, I would have to say yes.

Everyone's a Model

Supply and Demand

If you or anyone else is looking for a job right now, pick up your camera and go take a photography class. Why do I say this? Have you noticed how many people have professional head shots, photo shoots with their friends, action photos of them at work, rocking their favorite brands or sponsors, or modeling albums in their profiles? It seems like every person I know has at least one professionally produced photograph online. Why? Branding.

Images are extremely important in conveying a powerful brand. Individuals and companies are using images and also getting value from word-of-mouth sharing or, more accurately, word-of-photo share.

People learn and acquire information very differently. Most will have a strong reaction to images. Musicians, athletes, salespeople, high school students, and even rodeo clowns seem to understand that, and they are using it to their advantage. They are visually displaying their brand through images—and it's working. It's like flipping through a magazine and noticing the pictures and advertisements without reading the actual words. People are doing the same thing online with free media (social media).

These images convey messages of importance and status, and give insight into who these people really are. Everyone's a model. Go pick up a camera and start shooting.

$500 Fine and Loss of Client for Littering

One evening I was traveling home from work, heading north on A1A in semi-rush hour traffic. As I approached a soon-to-be red light, a work truck cut me off, causing me to jam pretty hard on my brakes. As we sat at the red light, the driver of the truck threw a cigarette butt out of the window. Now, I was already a little upset that he had cut me off, but throwing trash (yes, cigarette butts are trash) out of his window onto this beautiful stretch of Florida highway? That was too much. I became furious and wanted to yell at the guy, but I am a relatively peaceful person, plus the light turned green and he had already sped away.

As we came to the next traffic light, I was once again sitting directly behind the same vehicle. As we waited for the light to change, I noticed two interesting things. First, the vehicle had a "How's My Driving?" sticker. That actually made me laugh. The second was the fact that this truck was branded. The logo for his company, a lawn care company, was plastered all over the vehicle. I was actually in the market for lawn service and had planned on contacting this company originally. They were one of the best known at the beach, and I had seen their advertisements all over the place. Well, after what I witnessed from this employee, there was no way that I was going to contact them. I certainly didn't want the driver coming to my house!

It isn't just the leadership or high-profile employees at an organization that need to manage their brands. It is every single employee. Whether they are at the office, in front of a client, on a call, or driving around town, they are sending a message about who they are. This message can be very positive or extremely damaging. The market will take notice of the personal brands of your employees and tie that directly to your company.

It was too bad there wasn't a cop around during my trip home that day. The driver of the truck could have been stuck with a $500 fine for littering. Little did he or his company know.

CHAPTER 20

YOUR INTERNET

FOOTPRINT

Google It!

SiliconCloud is a leading global digital marketing firm. We help clients increase their Web traffic, convert that traffic into leads, and eventually turn those leads into clients. We help them grow their business by enhancing their Web presence.

One of our areas of expertise is search engine optimization (SEO). The value of SEO, as we see it, is twofold. First, we work to ensure that all of the results on page one from a search on a person or company are positive. Second, we help clients identify what search terms they want to be found for so they turn up in Internet search results even when potential customers are searching an industry or service, not for them specifically. Just as we do this for clients, we also do it for ourselves. If you search for "SiliconCloud," you will find all of the page one results positive and relevant. Because we are so good at managing what Google and other search engines think about us, we sometimes use the tagline "SiliconCloud—Google It!" My business partner, Patrick Murphy, has even logoed golf balls with the slogan. He figures every time someone finds one of his lost balls, they will read it, Google it, and find plenty of positive information on our company.

Just as potential customers search for our clients, and us, people are searching for you, as well! With Google and other search engines directing people to the most relevant information on the Web, it is now almost just as important to consider what Google thinks about you as what people think about you.

The idea of the Internet and search engines determining your brand is very real. There are stories now of parents choosing baby names based on available URLs. I'm serious! They won't name their baby "Patrick Sitkins," for example, since www.patricksitkins.com is already taken. It sounds a bit crazy, but it makes a lot of sense. What if your child becomes someone famous or high profile? They would certainly need a top-notch Web presence. But what if their name/domain was already taken? Well, someone could set up a negative site and post bad information, they could be an imposter posing as your child, or they could try to capitalize on the domain and attempt to sell it for big money. Parents now are very aware of the power of online brand management and Web presence, and they are taking proactive steps. Patrick Murphy told me about this right after my first son was born. So I'm sorry to the other Sitkins out there, but my son's name is now taken. I guess they will have to come up with another boy's name for their children!

If you are having a difficult time determining what your current brand is, there are a few very easy ways to find out. As mentioned above, doing an Internet search is the most common and well-known way. There is certainly a mentality of "I Google you, you Google me" out there. Have you really thought about the power in this? Without ever meeting you, people have the ability to know. It's as though the Internet and search engines have enabled the entire population to become private investigators. Within minutes, people can find out what you look like, where you work, your accomplishments, where you went to school, your interests, and your kids' names. They can do this all from the comfort of their couch, for free.

As if determining what you want people to think of you and managing that day-to-day isn't complex enough, now you have the Internet and technology to deal with.

Stalker

I always try to learn as much about someone as I can early on in a relationship. And why shouldn't I? The information is readily available.

One time I had an initial call with a potential client in Iowa. The conversation went fine and was very typical. There were a few quick pleasantries, such as "Tell me about your company," "What are you trying to get accomplished?" and so on. Nothing fantastic. Immediately after the call I pulled up a few social sites and requested to connect with him. Within a few hours we were "friends" on several sites.

After fifteen minutes of research, I knew that he was a Notre Dame graduate and a fanatical fan. I learned that he was married with two young kids. I discovered by his recent posts that he had just returned from a trip to the Dominican Republic and had stayed at the resort that was featured on my favorite outdoors show, *The Spanish Fly* with Jose Wejebe. I know knew more about this guy than I could have ever learned in multiple calls. He also had pictures from his agency, and I had a chance to get a feel for their work environment.

He was my new friend.

The next call went much differently. We chatted about his passions, and I talked about seeing the resort in the D.R. on *The Spanish Fly*. We had much more of a connection this time around than we did in the first call. No, knowing where he went to school and that he golfed in the D.R. did not automatically convince him to become a client. What it did do though was break down the barriers and allow us to talk as people, not faceless business drones on the other end of the phone.

I told this story at a sales leadership workshop in Boston, and my new "friend" Chris was in the audience. I was very open about the research that I had done and how it affected our relationship initially. At the end of my story he blurted out, "Man, you were kind of stalking me online . . . but it definitely worked."

Other Technology

One fantastic site is www.123people.com. This site pulls all of the information on you from the Internet and organizes it in a way so you can clearly see what you are telling people to think of you. All you have to do is type in your name, and within milliseconds your entire brand is displayed on one Web page. First, you may be overwhelmed and terrified at the detailed and accurate information that is displayed. Next, a sense of panic may occur when you see the type of information that is included. Your digital footprint shows images, videos, articles on or about you, recommendations, bios, products that you have developed or are associated with, your connections, your likes and dislikes, education, local involvement, tax records, [gulp] criminal records, your thoughts and conversations (blog), marriage and/or divorce records, social profiles, past jobs, and expertise. All of this is displayed elegantly on one page.

Probably the best function on the site is the tag cloud. This widget pulls the top keywords associated with your name. So after you have looked through all of the painstaking details about yourself, you are now presented with an even more rudimentary list at the bottom of the page. Talk about a swift kick to the stomach.

The silver lining in all of this is that it can be managed. If you are proactively managing your brand, playing good offense and defense, managing keywords, and optimizing technology, then this site should excite you. It will give you instant gratification, knowing that you are doing a great job managing your brand. On the other hand, it may be the wake-up call you've needed. You may run this report on yourself and be displeased with the results. Even worse, you could do the search and realize that it's not even information on you that comes back.

We have used this site with many of our clients and have run hundreds of tests. We have searched celebrities down to middle school-age kids. The two detrimental outcomes of poor information or misinformation are common. As an example, we ran an insurance agency CEO through the system. None—not a single item—of the information that came back was about him. We were hoping that some very clear, powerful words and information would show up. We were hoping that he was closely tied to his organization and vice versa. This was not the case. The images were of other people, tricycles, and other irrelevant objects. There were no correct contact options, and his tag cloud looked like it should be associated with Ami James from the show *NY Ink*. There were words like "tattoo," "tattoo shop," "photography," "foods," and other places and things that certainly do not describe him. What if a large prospect or insurance company connection searched him? What would they think about this CEO?

You may be thinking, *Well, maybe he has a very common name,* or, *He is secretly a tattoo enthusiast.* First, I can promise you that he does not and is not. Second, so what if he did have a common name? Should he just give up and assume that there is nothing he can do to fix this? Absolutely not. There are several ways to make the results for your name and your brand not only about you but also positive.

Try the site out for yourself. What if your name is John Smith or Jane Doe? Does that mean that you should just chalk up a bad Internet footprint to that? Or does it make sense to do everything in your power to make sure that you are the one who is attached to that name? To make sure that the information and media presented are about you?

"So Much Cooler Online"

If you are a country music fan, you probably remember the song by Brad Paisley titled "Online." In the song, Paisley describes a lovable loser who is a social outcast. But as the song progresses, he sings,

> Online I live in Malibu,
> I pose for Calvin Klein, I've been in *GQ*,
> I'm single and I'm rich,
> And I've got a set of six-pack abs that would blow your mind.

He continues on with a lot of statements about who he could be because he is hiding behind the computer.

The takeaway from this song shouldn't be to lie about your stats or be deceitful online. You have to be genuine in your message and brand no matter how you are communicating it. If you manufacture a false identity or brand, it may very well be discovered. A client may find out that you are not as experienced as you said you are, an employer will eventually find out that you aren't "as advertised," and, like the song above, a potential date will soon find out that your six-pack abs more closely resemble a keg.

However, the song does portray a very valuable (and, yes, comical) message about the power of online branding. If you manage you brand through different social media, websites, and other media, then you can, in fact, quickly manage your future brand. Again, we aren't suggesting that you portray a false image or information. What we are suggesting is that there is real power in speed and communicating your message through technology.

Six Pixels

In grade school, you probably heard about Frigyes Karinthy or at least his theory of six degrees of separation. In 1912, Frigyes Karinthy first developed the idea of six degrees of separation. His famous theory stated that everyone on the earth could be connected to any other person by a chain of no more than five acquaintances. Now, let's fast-forward a hundred years or so and introduce advanced technology to the equation. The Internet and social media applications have now shrunk the six degrees dramatically. We fully believe that you are no more than one or two connections away from anyone on the planet. Mitch Joel described this in his book *Six Pixels of Separation*. The subtitle "Everyone Is Connected. Connect Your Business to Everyone" certainly suggests that it is crucial for individuals and organizations to maximize their presence and optimize technology to work in their favor.

This idea of six pixels separating us all can be wildly optimistic, or it can also be devastatingly damaging. To echo earlier statements, if you believe that you are or could be proactively managing your brand online, then you will most likely see the six pixels as a great opportunity. If you are not managing your brand or Internet footprint, then you could be in serious trouble.

If you are truly one pixel or connection away from anyone, what does that mean? What if you could connect to the prospect you've been trying to meet, a decision maker at your dream job, an alumni that can get you into your school of choice, or someone famous? Oh, the possibilities! But if you can find them, then they can just as easily find you. What would happen if they did search for you? Would they find the person you truly are? Or would they find a damaging online version and a perception that screams *run*?

Managing your Internet footprint is certainly not the only way to manage your brand, but if you ignore it, your brand could quickly come crashing down.

Seven Types of Profiles

Matt Morehead is the CEO of Launch2Life, which is a program to help twenty-somethings get started in careers by understanding basic principles of finance, budgeting, insurance, networking, etc. He was sharing some thoughts with me about different profiles that he came up with to describe people. He shared them with me to get my thoughts and to develop those thoughts into this book. (Thanks, Matt!). Following are the profiles.

Tireless Self-Promoter
These individuals are constantly telling people about themselves. They often annoyingly promote their company, product, services, and philanthropic ventures. Instead of balancing personal and professional information, they tend to go overboard with their promotions. These people usually get hidden or removed as a connection altogether.

Never-Ending Christmas Letter

Before technology made it extremely easy for us to let people into our lives, we had to find other ways to let people know how we were and what we were up to. I can still remember my family getting the five-page letter in the envelope with the card. These letters were basically a year in review of the family sending the card. It was always funny to me. Why, since we never connect the other 364 days, are we interested in every aspect of your family's life now? The other thing I found humorous was how fabulous everyone was. Little Suzy has been accepted into Mensa, Johnny is the best player on his team, and the father of the family got a huge promotion at work. You never heard about the bad or mediocre stuff that happened during the year. It is the same online today.

Those in this group are constantly promoting how great their life is. Every day they are blessed because something amazing and wonderful happened. If you are like me, you know that bad stuff is happening to them—that's life. These people seem very fake and exaggerate.

Self-Appointed Motivator

This is the quote-of-the-day crowd. These people have taken the charge of motivating their entire friend circle online. They post quotes, spiritual sayings, and motivations to get through the workweek.

Attention Seeker

This is the FML crowd. If you don't know what FML stands for, you'll have to Google it.

This group of individuals always dramatizes everything that happens to them. I once saw a girl post, "The window in my new BMW 328i is stuck, so I am sitting in the service center getting it fixed—FML." Sure, car trouble is bothersome, but FML? Really? This made me sad for this girl. Her $37,000 car had trouble, and she had to sit in the service center that has catering and a full-time masseuse on staff. How horrible for her. Ninety-eight percent of the world would love to have that problem.

The Flame Thrower

This group is comprised of very opinionated people. They take every chance to comment and argue about politics, religion, sports, etc. These people tend to take things very seriously and can easily offend people.

The Voyeur

This group is out there, but they don't share anything. They either don't check their account very often, or they sit back and watch all the activity. This is a dangerous group to be in. We typically tell people to delete their account if that is their approach. It is more damaging to have an outdated or blank account than do nothing at all. They aren't using social media in the way that it is intended to be used—socially. You have to have a balance of give-and-take to be seen as an authority or relevant in the social media space.

Observer/Commenter

This is the group that gets it!

These people find ways to start and enter conversations. They comment on current events, repost useful information, balance the professional with the personal, and are always conscious of their personal brand. They understand how their interactions online can affect their brand, and they make decisions based on that.

They use social media to foster and maintain personal and professional relationships, establish their expertise and authority in the areas that they want to, and as a bonus oftentimes pick up new clients because of their efforts.

So which one are you?

Can you name a person to whom you are connected in each group? Does that support or damage their brand or your brand?

Larry's Take: Patrick is the real expert in this area. I have used him for numerous projects and strategies for my online presence.

Facebook is perceived by many people in 2013 as more of the personal social media versus business social media. I don't believe this is completely the case. I use my Facebook page as part of my business. More than half of my clients and many of my prospects are connected to me on Facebook. The depth of relationships with those people is incredible. It helps my ability to serve these clients when I know them more intimately through Facebook. I know it exposes my life and theirs. However, it deepens the relationship, and our businesses are positively impacted by this intimacy. Also, I have been purposefully looking at the frequency in which people recommend products, talk badly about products, refer to businesses in posts, and ask for recommendations on Facebook. About have of the posts on my Facebook home page mention a company or a product. Social media is the word of mouth of today! The word of mouth that comes through a "personal" site is frequent and powerful. I bet the initial sales of this book will be more influenced through Facebook than any other social media. I encourage you to think deeply about how all social media may play a role in your personal and business brand strategy.

CHAPTER 21

MY FINAL PLEA

I thought long and hard about how to end my section before we head into the Personal Branding Handbook section. *Should it be a quick review? Should I bring up one new idea? What if I beg them to take us seriously?* At the end of the day, it is your choice. There are obviously numerous stories and examples of how to enhance and damage your brand throughout this book. The facts are the facts.

We wrote this because of our success over the last several years, as well as the success of the people we've helped. We are convinced more than ever that personal branding is not only important but also a crucial strategy for anyone. We wanted to share this information with the market to truly help people. As someone who works daily on this for clients (and myself), I can tell you that this can get very overwhelming. I encourage you to implement some or most of the strategies that we've shared.

Our hope is to prevent brand damage for people we know, as well as for people with whom we can't directly consult.

Good luck!

THE PERSONAL BRANDING HANDBOOK FOR EVERYONE

We have worked with numerous types of people to help them with their brand. The following pages include ideas and examples of how you can create your brand. Just look for the topic that defines you the best, and get some ideas.

TEENS

High Volume Creates Higher Risk

Today's teenagers are the masters of technology usage. They are naturally talented at making the handheld device a part of their life. They sleep with their phone, type faster on their phone than adults can on a keyboard, carry on multiple conversations at the same time, make photography into communication, and think video is part of daily life.

These skills and behaviors are changing our world, and everyone will need to get on board if they want to be relevant in the future. This group is establishing our new norms.

However, they are also at the highest risk of a big fall. They are at high risk of bullying, slander, mistakes, and potentially lifelong brand damage with every move they make. The mental side of this technology use has to be their guide.

My daughters are all doing a very good job of this (I continue to pray). They think about their brand and make it part of their daily language. They have shared the branding concept with their friends, and it has become a common language for them. If teenagers and their friends are all aware of how technology will impact their brand, they will do a better job of protecting that brand. This group can watch out for each other.

If they think of technology as a broadcasting device that is telling everyone what to think of them, they will have a chance of successfully managing their brand. Even if they are on a video with someone, realizing the other person may be recording them can be a great mind-set. We never know if the person on the other side of the video may have someone else in the room, listening to what we are saying. This happened recently to a friend of mine. He thought he was one-on-one in a video chat. He didn't realize someone he was talking about was sitting in the room out of the range of the camera. Big brand damage!

Teenagers need to make technology a resource to promote a powerful brand. It is great media to project what they want people to think.

They also need to keep in mind that we live in a technology world where their brand will stay with them for a while. Whatever they do today will stay with them in the future. Every decision they make could have long-lasting effects. So they should be aware and manage the risk.

COLLEGE

Launching to Life

There are certain things that the traditional university lacks when it comes to developing young professionals. Parents, business owners, and managers are seeing more and more graduates ill-equipped with the necessary tools to handle their transition to the post-scholastic phase. This is extremely concerning.

One company has taken this problem head-on and created a program to deal with it. Our good friend Matt Morehead created Launch2Life, a development program for twenty-somethings. The program gives young adults financial planning, network building, résumé writing, and interview skills, and they even help them craft their brand. We sat down with Matt to discuss what separated the successful graduates from the not-so-successful ones. He was kind enough to walk us through the information he presents during his professional presence sessions. We began our discussion around the fact that everyone has a brand. We joked and equated it to pregnancy—you can't be *kind of* pregnant. You either are or you aren't. The same goes for your personal brand or, as he describes it, your professional presence. Once he drives that point home, he then helps them examine what people think of them by walking them through a series of questions. He asks them if they are seen as

- someone who is polished and "put together" or someone who's a mess;

- someone who consistently maintains a high level of energy or someone who has major mood and energy swings;
- someone who is confident or someone who lacks confidence;
- someone who is grateful and appreciative or someone who has an entitlement mentality;
- someone who is fun and interesting to be around or someone who is boring and brings very little to each interaction;
- someone who is always on time and ready to go or someone who shows up consistently late and underprepared;
- someone who is organized or someone who is disorganized;
- someone who takes care of his/her health, nutrition, and appearance or someone who is out of shape and sloppy with his/her appearance;
- someone who talks first and listens second or someone who listens first and talks second;
- someone who drinks and socializes responsibly or someone who loses control;
- and someone who spends their money frivolously or someone who is careful with their money.

Notice the above questions are about character traits, not skills. Skills can certainly be a part of your brand, but your personal brand goes much deeper than that. Skills and knowledge are assumed. They are what got you into the school of your choice or your job. Your true brand is more than skills and intellect; it is your reputation. If you are having a hard time defining your brand, seek out those who have seen and interacted with you frequently over a significant period of time (a year or more) and are not family members. I did this very early in my career. Looking at myself and trying to think about my brand and reputation was very difficult. I asked Dianne, one of my best friends from high school, an old coach, a coworker, and my dad what they believed my unique abilities to be. It was extremely beneficial to get their input. It was great to see that my thoughts and what they saw were in alignment. I also saw items that I had never really considered to be who I am. I took a few of those and worked hard to incorporate them into my brand. Discovering your current brand begins by having the courage to interrogate your reality.

All of us can craft a personal brand over a short period of time by giving new acquaintances a first impression of who we are. However, a true personal brand is about who we are day in and day out. So what if you don't like your current brand? Can you change it? Absolutely, but it can take many years. Being a young person just starting out is actually a huge advantage in the personal branding space. Your slate is largely clean except for what a few friends and acquaintances know about you. Most of these people will have little effect on your future. Yes, there are things that can permanently damage your brand, but you can develop the brand you want much more easily early on in life and in your career.

Matt told us that he sometimes gets feedback from young people. "I don't want to live my life worrying about what others think of me. I just want to be myself. If they don't like that, then tough." Personal brand and professional presence aren't about us all conforming. Again, your brand has to differentiate you. It is certainly about being an individual and being yourself.

You get to choose the elements of your brand. You will always have people in this world who don't like you and will judge you unfairly. That's part of life. Personal brand is about being genuine and consistent. Authentic relationships are built on consistency. I can't build a great relationship with you if I don't know what I am going to get from one interaction to the next.

If I know who you are (through your brand), I can first decide to form a relationship with you or not and then adapt my interactions with you based on your brand. I know what I am getting. Personal brand also tells me about your judgment. From what you post online to what you choose to wear to meetings, I get to assess your judgment. Do I trust your judgment? If I'm your employer, do I trust your judgment enough to allow you to interact with my best clients?

We once had an employee who was loved by many of our clients. This person was outgoing, helpful, and fun at events. A little too fun. We started noticing behavior and getting feedback from clients that was very negative and certainly against the brand Larry and I were building at our company. Stories of inappropriate behavior and partying began to circulate amongst our clients. We approached this employee several times and attempted to help her manage her personal brand more effectively. Unfortunately, this employee could not effectively manage her professional presence. Because of this, we were not comfortable placing her in front of clients. After a large investment of time and energy, we knew that this employee was not willing to change, and our trust in her had been damaged beyond repair. We eventually had to let her go.

You Have to Earn the Right

Just as we discussed above, we tend to get feedback from young people who say that they want to just be themselves. They don't care what people think about them. They want to be free to express themselves, just like Mark Zuckerberg. Yes, we get that reference a lot.

Let's think about this for a second. Yes, Mark is very open and honest, and he really doesn't care what people think about him. There is a reason. He's earned the right to think that way. We believe that there is a direct link between what you've accomplished in life and what you can get away with. Another way to say this is your level of self-expression has to be in alignment with your accomplishments.

There is a hierarchy. If you are in a school organization, team, company, or any group, you have seen this phenomenon. The higher up in a social structure, the more you can get away with. The status of a person is directly related to the amount of shenanigans that are tolerated. These shenanigans can be things like relaxed schedule, conformity to the rules, jokes and statements that are allowed, loudly communicating an opinion, interaction with authority, etc. The reason that these people tend to get away with more is simple. They have earned the right.

Early on at Jacksonville University and then later on when I was starting my career, I was extremely reserved. I would only insert my thoughts or opinions when forced. I toned down what I did online, kept my private life extremely quiet, and didn't really let people know who I was. Looking back, it may have been a bit extreme, but my reasoning was that I hadn't earned the right. I had to prove my value to the team and the organization. Senior classmen to me had proven themselves and could be more animated, opinionated, and visible. I was just one of three freshmen on the team. It was tough to be taken seriously, until season came. I began to form stronger relationships and let my true personality show, but only after making the travel squad and actually getting some playing time. The same went with my career. I was surrounded by high-level executives as partners and clients. It wasn't until I had proven my value that I could start to express myself a little more and let people in. There are certainly things that I do, say, and express now that I wouldn't have even dreamed of early on. These things aren't bad; they are just opinions. I feel like I've earned the right to say the things I do and act the way I do. It's not easy to get to that place though.

Right on the Cusp

Those of us who escaped the both awesome and terrifying social networking age in our younger years often wonder what life would have been like if all this technology had been around when we were in college. Would dating have been a lot easier? Could class notes be shared on a larger scale? Could we have all known what was going on all over campus? Those would have been cool things to have, but what about the damage this could create? Posted pictures of the baseball initiation party, a video of your twenty-first birthday recorded on a smartphone and posted to YouTube, a late-night post on that soccer girl's wall that you forgot about till the next morning, your parents finding out about your speeding ticket or new tattoo via Twitter—oh, the humanity! Fortunately for my peer group, these were not possible. Unfortunately for today's college-age student, it's a reality.

We often jokingly say, "Thank god that stuff wasn't around when we were in school." We weren't that wild of a group (not any more than any other college kids). The part that scares us is that we wouldn't have had a clue how to manage all of this. Some of our youthful mistakes could be much more than memories today. With technology and the way information is shared, these could very easily be relived via a variety of media.

With Great Power Comes Great Responsibility

Yoda was right.

As a college student, you have had access to and will continue to see the creation of powerful technology, media, and tools to help you. Many of these will directly affect your brand. As illustrated above, many of your choices, interactions, and communications can quickly become public information. It is up to you to utilize these tools to positively communicate your reputation.

Brand management is not solely technology driven. It may be easy for a tech-savvy student to "manage the press" by untagging pictures and deleting damaging content, but what about your reputation? This goes far beyond technology.

You have probably heard the phrase, "It's not what you know, it's who you know." This is an extremely accurate statement. We are not suggesting that just knowing people will help you succeed post-college; however, it certainly helps. You never know who will be able to help you down the line. It could be a professor, a coach, a roommate, a friend's parent, etc. Since anyone could possibly be a great connection later on, it seems logical that you should start managing what people think of you now.

Branding isn't something that you can put off till after graduation. You need to start now. Think about who you are currently and, more importantly, who you want to be. Ask yourself how you can develop into that. What resources will you need? Who do you know that could help you get there? Who could be a possible mentor? What things support your current and future brand? What could damage your brand slightly? What could have a lasting negative effect?

College is a fantastic time of growth, learning, and development. Don't waste the knowledge, interactions, and social environment. You can learn a lot about what you want and what you need to avoid.

FAMILY

The Family Impacts the Individuals

A family has a brand just like a person does. I have seen family brands keep kids from being successful, and I have seen family brands create opportunities. A family brand has a huge impact on the opportunities presented to and eliminated from that family.

I have seen coaches not want kids on teams because of the brand of a family. I have seen kids put on teams because of the family brand. This is true for sports, music, dance, church activities, school programs, and more. Your family brand can be a powerful thing to manage.

How do we manage a family brand? Here you go.

1. Sit down as a family, and determine what you want your brand items to be. You will basically answer the question, "What do we want people to think of us as a family?" The answers will be things like hardworking, honest, selfless, caring, philanthropic, etc.

2. Remember that language drives culture. Parents and kids have to consistently use language that supports that brand. In our family, "inclusion of others" is a value and a brand item we desire. So we talk about inclusion frequently in our home. We challenge our kids when we feel they are not including others. The frequency of the language will drive the behaviors.

3. Revisit your brand, and talk about how it is being applied in each person's life outside of the home. If each person has to tell one thing they did this week to make our brand a reality, they will be

focused on it more often. It will also give you a chance to celebrate when a family member does something in line with your desired brand.

4. Quickly eliminate items that conflict with your brand. If you send a conflicting message to others, it will damage your brand. So in the name of brand management, correct items that contrast. This will actually be easier now, because you will be working on the brand and not attacking the individual.

5. If you revisit every year (make it a New Year's activity), you will keep it fresh and sharp and be able to celebrate what you have accomplished in the past.

EARLY CAREER

Managing Perceptions

The early stages of a career are a whirlwind. You have to learn the culture of the organization and how to fit in. There is technical training, business acumen development, organizational skills to develop, contacts to make, meetings to attend, and all of this while trying to prove your value as early as possible. If you are lucky, management will have you in a development program, and they may even have put a plan together with you. We've noticed that personal branding, and management of it, is rarely focused on. Because it is rarely focused on, people early in their careers typically don't see the value in it, or they may think brand management is something for those high up in the organization. Maybe only top producers and key executives need to worry about their personal brand. They may think, *All I have to do is work hard and do a good job.* Well, first let's look at the reality of your situation.

Your Perception

This organization is lucky to have me. I am going to bring some youthful energy to this stagnant organization. I'll be able to use all this new knowledge. I've got a great opportunity to learn from some of the successful people here. I am going to set the world on fire. I'm going to make a difference. This is awesome!

Your Coworkers' and Managers' Perception

Great, another person to train. They are going to need so much attention up front. I really don't have time for this. This investment better work out. Someone is going to have to show them the ropes. I wonder how long this one will last. Someone needs to break this kid of youthful tendencies.

If You're Related to Anyone in Leadership or Ownership

Amplify doubts about you times ten. Increase hurdles to overcome times ten. Increase the amount of work it will take to effectively manage a positive and powerful brand times ten.

Are You Essential?

The marketplace was much different when I began working with Larry back in 2006. Back then there was a free agent-type mentality among employees, especially recent graduates. Companies were investing time, resources, and capital in becoming the employer of choice. Top organizations were focusing almost as much time on recruiting top talent as they were on marketing to potential clients. Around 2008, the market changed dramatically. The free agency market dried up, and suddenly recent grads, as well as seasoned pros, were finding it harder and harder to find and keep a steady job.

We've all heard stories of top executives suddenly without work and applying for entry-level positions, or the college grads who are still living at home because they can't do anything with their degree. Unemployment rates continue to bounce around but remain exceedingly high, especially in the United States, and uncertainty of global economies is going to continue to be a challenge. So what can you do to find a job and keep it if you don't already have one, or maintain or advance your position at your current company? In other words, how can you become essential? Certainly results and excellent performance will help. What about your brand? Do you think it could help you stand out from the crowd? If done correctly, yes, and this will be essential early on in your career. There are several reasons for this.

First, you need to make yourself one of the most valuable assets on the team (or at least be perceived that way) in case of another major downturn in the market. If you manage a positive and powerful brand internally, people will be more willing to help you and fight to keep you around.

Try reaching out to help others, especially early on. The old saying is true: "They don't care how much you know, until they know how much you care."

You will have a lot of challenges to overcome. Purposefully managing your brand and showing perceived value will help you overcome some of these.

If you have a strong brand it will set you apart with your clients, vendors, prospects, and centers of influence. Again, results and performance will be key early on. Purposefully managing your brand will help.

We have worked with thousands of individuals in different industries and at different levels of their careers. As mentioned earlier, we used to run a program for salespeople in their early twenties to late thirties. Most of them had been with their company less than a month, and in some cases the class was their first day on the job. We had one person say, "I don't even know where my desk is."

We became very good at spotting those who had "it" and those who didn't. Those who had "it" could typically look at themselves and identify their natural talents, value, differentiation, and future brand. They could take their brand and truly manage what others (employees, clients, prospects, and centers of influence) thought of them. It was truly a foundation for their success.

Over the four years of running the class, Larry and I kept an informal list of those participants who had "it," the ones we knew would be successful. Not all of them stayed in the sector they were in, but all of them are still very successful in their career.

Professional Presence

This is an extremely important element in your personal presence, especially early on in your career. Professional presence is the way you present yourself verbally, in writing, online, and visually. All four areas have to be managed in order to maintain a strong personal brand inside of your organization and in the marketplace.

Verbal

Managing your professional presence while speaking is more than the words that you are saying. It's about your interaction, tone, posture, and listening skills. Without the proper mix, it won't matter what you have to say. Here are some things to consider:

- Look people in the eye when speaking and listening.
- *Like, no youthful words, um, okay? Totally, you know?*
- Actively listen and respond appropriately.
- Show a general interest in your audience.
- Be interesting by telling stories.
- Be relentlessly prepared.
- Use tone and posture to enhance your words.

Written

Writing has become a lost art. Sure, you took basic grammar, language, and writing courses at some point in school, but are you prepared to communicate effectively in the professional world? Unfortunately, technology is damaging our ability to correctly communicate. Texting, e-mailing, and IM'ing have brought about a new language specific to the technology. These are not appropriate in the business world (most times). Follow these guidelines:

- Be concise, but give all of the information requested or needed.
- LOL! No abbreviations. My father-in-law, Tom, is not the most tech-savvy individual at times. For months, a new, younger

employee of his used the LOL abbreviation a lot in his e-mail communications. One day, Tom made an offhand comment to someone else in his office about the new employee. He said, "This is a bit inappropriate. In a lot of his e-mails, he says, 'Lots of love.'" Needless to say, Tom's coworker got a kick out of this when she explained to him that LOL meant "Laugh out loud." Our family still likes to joke with him about this. Don't assume that everyone knows what you are trying to say with abbreviations, especially in more formal communications.

- Always treat e-mails like actual letters. Assume that your communication will get passed around.
- Personality is okay, but make sure you keep your tone professional.

Online

We addressed this subject earlier in the book. There are some specific items to include for the early-career group.

- Never complain about your work situation, supervisors, hours, etc.
- A balance of personal and professional information, posts, images, etc., is best.
- Avoid controversial opinions unless you have accurate information, are ready to back them up, and can stand your ground. Examples of controversial topics include politics, religion, sexual orientation, etc.
- Your profiles very clearly communicate your brand. Proactively manage them.
- Determine what type of profile you have (from the section titled Seven Types of Profiles).

Visual

This is another way to proactively manage your brand. As mentioned early on, it takes only thirty seconds (eight for women) to form an opinion of you. Others will then spend the rest of the relationship finding examples to support their initial impression. Here are some items to keep in mind:

- How you dress. We teach people to dress half up from their audience. This can be at work, at dinner, for leisure, at the gym, etc.
- Be sharp, but blend.
- Arrive on time (preferably a few minutes early).
- Take notes when someone is talking to you.
- Create mass and space. Stand up tall, and project confidence.
- Early in your career you will find a lot of challenges and obstacles to overcome. If you manage your personal brand effectively, then you will have a greater chance at success.

Seasoned Pro

The Learning Cycle

Some years ago I was introduced to the four stages of competence, which is used in understanding the cycle of learning. The concept was originally developed by Abraham Maslow (though not recognized in his major works), but was later developed at Gordon Training International by its employee Noel Burch in the 1970s. Let me give a quick overview.

In learning, we go through four stages: unconscious incompetence, conscious incompetence, conscious competence, and unconscious competence.

Unconscious incompetence. We don't know what we don't know. This became very evident to me as I listened to my fourteen-year-old daughter talk about how easy it is going to be when she gets to drive. "I am going to be a great driver, Dad! It is so easy."

Conscious incompetence. We know that we are incompetent. The other day my fifteen-year-old daughter received her learner's permit and got behind the wheel, and she was conscious incompetent. She had no idea what to do, and she and I both knew we were in danger in that moment. This person needs practice to go to the next phase.

Conscious competence. When my daughter drove for a few weeks with her learner's permit, she had to think about every move she made. She is safe and capable. I can see why they don't just give fifteen-year-olds a license to drive. These people don't need practice; they need pressure. As they receive real-world pressure on what they have practices, they will learn to do things without having to think.

Unconscious competence. This is what many drivers eventually become. I can't say all, because I am amazed daily at the drivers' abilities. However, when you no longer have to think about what you are doing, and you have mastered the skill, you are unconsciously competent. This is the phase we all hope to reach in all areas we choose to learn.

Okay, so what in the world does this have to do with branding? The final phase doesn't end at unconscious competence. The process is actually a circle. The next phase is unconscious incompetence. This is what we see from many seasoned pros. They start looking at themselves as all-knowing experts. They don't need to learn anything new. The ego of these individuals is so large that they would not want anyone to see weakness in their game.

In a world where information is moving faster than at any time in history, the brand of many of these individuals becomes very negative very fast. These are the people who others roll their eyes at when they think of them. They feel sorry for them because they are stuck in the past.

Seasoned pros' biggest challenge is to stay on top of their game. If you're a seasoned pro, don't get lazy. Don't let your past success keep you from finding new success.

Your brand needs to be managed by reading current information, writing blogs about topics and articles, and giving your opinions. You need to be opening new files in the minds of the readers that others haven't thought about in your world of expertise. Look for something new. Look for something to innovate in your area of passion. Make everyone else continue to chase you. Use technology, and embrace the many possible ways of improving your skills.

If you can avoid being branded as "old school" or "out-of-date," you will stand out from the rest and will never have people roll their eyes at you.

END OF CAREER

"Come on, Grandma!"

I had a very good friend tell me he cringes every time his grandma posts anything on social media. He said, "She thinks that she is talking to her friends in the kitchen and doesn't realize her audience."

When I turned forty, I changed my perspective on life. I started to not care what people thought of me as much as I had in the past. I became a little more opinionated and started choosing whom I wanted to please.

When I turned fifty, I changed my perspective on life. I completely didn't care what others thought about me. I was accomplished and successful and just didn't have the time to worry about those who didn't agree with me or didn't like me.

I have heard that when I turn sixty, I will change my perspective again. I will stop caring that others have an opinion about me.

These generalizations are a bit overstated, but they are certainly close to the way my mind works. Our age gives us confidence, and our successes make caring about others' thoughts about us a little less important. Wisdom says, "I can't change what others think of me."

Now for reality. We live in a world where information is readily accessible. We used to be able to retire and move on and live in our small community that agreed with us. This isn't how it works in the modern world. Now we have social media and video capabilities that are expanding our footprint and our world. So we have to do some things differently if we want to engage with those in our lives. You may not "care" about what I am saying here, but if you do, here are some ideas for great brand management:

1. Realize that social media is bigger than you think. If you wouldn't say something at a country club party, where you don't know everyone who is there, don't say it on a social media site. It is not your safe place. You can quickly offend people if you decide to speak as freely there as you do in your kitchen with close friends. You can't control who sees what, and you will miss a lot of feedback (what they say about you when they read it). Keep your comments positive, and look at others' information. Make a game of it. See if you can learn about generations and what is important to them by reading what they post on their sites. My wife and I are "friends" on Facebook with a lot of our kids' friends. We rarely post anything on their comments or status. So they kind of forget we are there. Makes for great intel!

2. Read current events. The better you understand what is going on in the world, the more relevant you will be. Be interesting by knowing what is going on in the world around you.

3. Read something every week that has the opposing view. This will help you understand others. Seek to understand before seeking to be understood. I didn't invent it, but I sure use the idea a lot.

4. Ask a lot of questions, and continue to learn. I don't know this for a fact, but I have heard you can continue to learn into your eighties (and remember what you learned). However, many people stop learning, and the brain atrophies. Keep learning, and you will have a brand that others will want to engage.

5. Smile. Too many people who retire stop smiling. Be happy, and let others know you are happy. I know you may be tired, but a warm smile will engage and welcome others.

SUMMARY

This project has taken us over a year to write, because every time we get close to publishing we find another change in technology or new concepts in personal branding. Personal branding is evolving quickly and is having a stronger impact today than when we started the book. Personal branding is going to multiply over the next few years into a common practice. When the Internet started, I am certain that nobody could have predicted where we would be today in how our personal brands would be impacted. I am also certain we don't know how clear those brands will be a few years from today. I am also certain that if you are random with the management of your brand, it has a great chance of being damaged.

We hope this journey through personal branding has given you some insight and strategies to build and manage your brand. What you learned here may be obsolete in a few months. It is almost certain that new technology will have been innovated and available to impact your brand. We hope you are accepting it and finding ways to make it work for you.

Hundreds of books will be written on this topic, and strategies will change. We believe the core concepts of proactive brand management and identifying what you want people to think of when they think of you will never go away.

We hope you will be one who avoids *brand damage*!

Michael in Uganda teaching his students about personal branding.

CPSIA information can be obtained at www.ICGtesting.com
Printed in the USA
BVOW070008160713

325999BV00001B/1/P